£2.50

D0297896

CJ

CJ

The Autobiography of
C J de Mooi

MY JOURNEY FROM THE STREETS
TO THE SCREEN

JOHN BLAKE

Published by John Blake Publishing Ltd,
3 Bramber Court, 2 Bramber Road,
London W14 9PB, England

www.johnblakebooks.com

www.facebook.com/johnblakebooks 🆕
twitter.com/jblakebooks 🅴

This edition published in 2015

ISBN: 978 1 78418 711 8

British Library Cataloguing-in-Publication Data:

A catalogue record for this book is available from the British Library.

Design by www.envydesign.co.uk

Printed in Great Britain by CPI Group (UK) Ltd

1 3 5 7 9 10 8 6 4 2

Papers used by John Blake Publishing are natural, recyclable products made
from wood grown in sustainable forests. The manufacturing processes conform
to the environmental regulations of the country of origin.

Every attempt has been made to contact the relevant copyright-holders,
but some were unobtainable. We would be grateful if the
appropriate people could contact us.

For Andrew – as with everything in my life.

Very special thanks to:
Jack Thorpe-Baker
Jayne Barker
Adam Croft
Steve Mottershead
Jeremy Vine

CONTENTS

CONTENTS

INTRODUCTION

So many people have asked (or occasionally pestered) me to write this book, but I always used to find excuses or clumsily change the subject.

The main reasons for this all stemmed from the same root. My childhood was extremely traumatic, and I really didn't want to start digging into old memories and emotions. I was afraid to reawaken long-buried feelings of misery or overwhelming helplessness. Because of the nature of my early years, I'd deliberately and very successfully suppressed most of what had happened. Some things, of course, were seared into my mind, but the majority had been locked away or forgotten. The sadness was so intense and long lasting, I'm sure it would otherwise have become pure, uncontrollable rage.

A very secure defence mechanism was the only way I was going to survive. It was necessary to protect myself and, indeed, others. Revenge has never been my style, and I simply can't understand the need for it, even when it's dressed up in the implausible cloak of justice. I'll never comprehend those who turn to aggression as a first resort, but then maturity in age is never a guarantee of maturity in attitude. Without this level of personal management I doubt I'd be alive today; or if I were, then a jail or mental hospital might be my most likely home.

I won't over-dramatise the situation, but I will be brutally, and maybe uncomfortably, honest, because it really was that bad. Sorry if you thought this book was going to be a light-hearted romp through a few quiz shows, some garish shirts and a mindboggling array of hairstyles. We will, of course, get to all that later, but in order for me to survive and reach those brighter times, I had to go through hell.

Having finally decided to go ahead with this book, I faced an unexpected question: why exactly am I writing it? Am I really going to try to persuade you that it's some grand cathartic experiment? Or might it be helpful to impart my firsthand experiences of homelessness, near-suicide, prostitution and crime to others? Well, perhaps yes, even if it all accounts for only a mere sliver of the truth.

Over the previous few years, I've been bombarded with requests to talk about my life, but they never carried enough of an incentive. However, I am a pragmatist and I understand that such a book, while sensational in the truest sense of the word, could help my professional profile. A percentage of the monies from my previous book, *How to Win TV Quiz Shows*, were donated to a charity of which I am a patron. Therefore, I could realistically hope for some remuneration this time round that might benefit other causes, as well as my own bank account. This may seem selfish, but I've already said I'm not going to be anything less than directly open and honest. It wouldn't be me if I were anything but.

I guess there's no clear-cut answer for why I now feel ready to talk about what were previously taboo topics. I could have been considerably more visceral in my portrayals of certain people and still not come close to what they deserved. Abusing, hurting or dismissing children is always unacceptable. Alas, there are people in every walk of life, and even in positions of trust, who choose to ignore this. Detachment and disdain can be powerful shields to those who may not think their actions – or their indifference – qualify as abuse. But I barely lived through it all, and I can testify to the effects of their attitudes.

I hope you enjoy my story – or at least come to understand it. It might not make for easy reading to start with, but, fortunately, it does grow sunnier over time. Tragically, many people never get to enjoy such brighter skies. This book is dedicated to them.

CJ de Mooi
April 2015

1

GROWING UP

I loathed almost every single second of my childhood. I was born to parents Peter and Mary, for whom I was an inconvenient burden, and both made it perfectly clear every day, in words and actions, that they neither loved nor cared about me.

Now that may seem like a cavalier way to start an autobiography, but what else would you prefer I do? Sugarcoat it as something nicer than it was? *Oh CJ, you might think, you were too young to understand. You got it all wrong, you silly boy!*

Really? They told me to my face from a very early age that they didn't want me, like me or trust me. I heard this repeatedly throughout my entire childhood. I'm sorry, but that's as plain as I can make it.

They often told me I should be taken away and put into care. So many nights I wished for this to come true. At least once, I could have done with knowing what 'care' was. For the first decade and a half I spent with those people, I only ever recall being sad and scared. The fury came later.

*   *   *

I was born in Barnsley on 5 November 1969. I always thought this was rather unfair. Couldn't they have waited a few measly weeks so I could be a hip child of the 1970s?

Andrew Paul: that's the name I was given. When I was young, I was unsure if I despised the name in itself, or because it was a daily reminder of those who gave it to me; it took a while to grasp it was the latter. Ironically, 'Andrew' later became the most important name to me in the world. However, I spent the first nineteen years of my life dreading being addressed in person.

My earliest definite memory is of nursery school when I was three. It was photo day and I was dressed in grey trousers and chunky brown cardigan; maybe my later penchant for colourful shirts was just making up for sartorial lost time. I'd apparently already gained a reputation for being withdrawn and miserable. The teacher openly mocked me with the name 'Smiler' and coaxed the other children to do likewise.

The reason this day remains with me is because something had gone missing from the classroom, and the teacher immediately turned on me. Whether this was based on her prejudice or something another child had said, I don't know, but I was directly accused.

I knew nothing about any theft, but this injustice stayed with me and sowed the seed of my inherent mistrust of anyone in so-called authority. It was not the last time a finger would be wrongly – and viciously – pointed at me.

I have a vague mental image of a semi-detached house on a Barnsley cul-de-sac. I'm pretty sure it was real but, as so much of my memory has been lost, let's assume it was one of the fragments that remain resolutely intact. I can picture an unremarkably plain-looking house with a car on the driveway; we lived in the left half. The lounge was at the front with a fireplace and a couple of sofas, which overlooked a small lawn sloping down to the road.

And that, I'm afraid, is pretty much the extent of what I know about the first five years of my life. My formative years are reduced to a handful of ghostly images and even fewer hazy events. I know most people lack a crystal-clear, celluloid storyline of their young lives, but this must surely be unusual by any standards?

When I was four, the household moved to Rotherham. (I can't bring myself to use the word 'family', as we were anything but.) It was an outwardly respectable, detached, middle-class house on a new and relatively affluent estate. It was just the sort of place for twitching curtains and hypocritically averted gazes if anything untoward happened. At all costs, one must avoid upsetting the fragile suburban applecart!

I can see glimpses of a private preparatory school I may have attended for a year when I was about seven. This was no mere childhood dream, as I know the school exists, and can recall the yard, lunch hall and music room. It was my first experience of a school uniform, a feeling I absolutely adored. My attachment to these outfits tickles me now, as I feel really out of place even in a casual suit. Tuxedos and formal attire are my idea of purgatory! But I wonder if it wasn't so much the clothes themselves I liked, but rather the feeling of a single point of constancy in an ever-changing and confusing world.

As many young boys do, I became fascinated by dinosaurs and read about them with incessant fervour. I loved their variety and exotic nature but, with the benefit of hindsight, it was probably their remoteness I found most intriguing. Impassive creatures inhabiting a world so far away it was unreachable; science fact in essence becomes science fiction.

I was obviously destined to become a geek and, with dinosaurs, I had discovered my personal Nerdvana! I learned all their names and characteristics, but especially enjoyed studying their evolutionary differences. 'Lizard-hipped' was also a favourite phrase; it would resurface fortuitously as the answer to my very last *Eggheads* question before my two-year hiatus, a mere third of a century later!

Prehistory proved a passing fancy, although I made quite sure I learned the word 'palaeontology'. This was, of course, just for my personal reference and not at all to show off in conversation (Pretentious, *moi?*). It did, however, spark into life my love of learning. I had a battered old illustrated encyclopaedia I delved into every day, which had one very odd quirk in that the articles were arranged as to which would appeal to boys and which to girls. I found this very strange and it made me uncomfortable, although I wasn't sure why. Bizarrely, apart from a lone entry on the Bowie knife (which apparently only boys would be interested in), every single listing was recommended for both sexes. So what, exactly, was the point of that?

The local comprehensive infants school followed, and I quickly realised that I loved *learning* rather than being taught. Throughout the next eight years, I don't think I ever met a teacher who was truly passionate about the job. We were being processed like mindless cattle merely to pass the school's exams. This may have been the fault of the governing authority, or due to a lacklustre and disengaged workforce, but every day this conveyor belt continued without inspiration. The subjects on offer were bland and of little practical use once our school lives were over. Basic finance, social skills, relationship advice... where were the texts children could actually use and apply in later life? After all these years, I've yet to find a single elusive soul for whom quadratic equations represented a scholastic high point.

One issue I felt unable to discuss was the fact that I considered myself more intelligent than most of the people around me, irrespective of age. I was already aware that mental acuity had nothing to do with how old someone was and that it remained fairly constant through life. Misconceptions about this always bug me, and I'm reminded of my appearance on *The Weakest Link*. I got a question wrong and Anne Robinson commented I should have been more intelligent. I immediately shot back that it had nothing to do with intelligence, merely knowledge, and if *she* had been more intelligent she would have realised that. The show quickly moved on and the interchange was predictably cut from the final edit.

I could never shake the feeling a lot of educators were there because they possessed the one vital skill necessary to teach children: all they were required to do was stay one

5

lesson ahead of those in their charge. I yearned to go so much further but was bound by the stifling boundaries of an unimaginative curriculum.

I now rejoice that my mind is free to explore whatever I want. I've learned exponentially more since leaving formal (and I use that word very purposefully) education. In recent years I've also had the opportunity to visit plenty of schools, and I'm delighted to see that both the quality and the freedom inherent within education have definitely improved. That's not to say bad teachers don't remain, of course they do, but the minority is now thankfully outnumbered. Many tutors are still frustrated by the limits imposed upon them, but they honestly want children to be fascinated by what they're learning. Education is an invaluable keystone, but real advancement only comes with the encouragement of independent thought.

The brain is an incredible entity and it's a great shame to waste it. We are here for an infinitesimally brief flicker of time, and I for one am going to make the most of it. I'm repeatedly asked why I'm so active and my reply is invariably the same: in my one short life on this floating rock, I'm going to do much as I can. I'll have plenty of time to rest when I'm dead, but I categorically refuse to be lying on my deathbed thinking, *What if...?* If I'm ever to have regrets, they'll be for the chances I grabbed with both hands rather than for the opportunities I let slip through my fingers. Life is for living, dammit!

Nevertheless, during my incarceration at primary school there was a single enjoyable moment that proved to be the first step of a journey, as yet still incomplete. Admittedly, that journey would be rudely interrupted for twenty-five years, but as the eventual second step led me to my one true passion, it was worth the extended wait.

The school staged a production of a musical revue called *Rooster Rag*, and I was cast in the lead role. I have no idea why this chance befell me, as I don't recall any previous performances, so perhaps it was, as so many revelations are, pure serendipity.

It was a typical piece of fluff that built to a dramatic crescendo where I was throttled by a fox during my big solo. What a way to go! But my love of performing was born, and from that moment I recognised the stage as where I wanted to spend the rest of my life. Some people want to be actors, but others – myself very much included – *need* to be actors. It's the only thing that will ever make us happy or fulfilled. It's not just *in* our blood; it *is* the very lifeblood that maintains us.

Only twice in my life have I faced a major decision that required not even a split second of contemplation. Both were deep, almost sensual and life changing: the first was the decision to become an actor; and the second took place when I met my partner. Both were moments that elicited an instant and unconditional love. Each demanded total devotion, and I wasn't prepared to deny or lie to myself about either. At eight years old I became an actor and was certain that, whatever became of my life, I would always remain so. Having a direction and desperately hanging onto it would save me countless times from what lay ahead.

I joined a local dramatic company and performed in several plays over the ensuing few years at the Rotherham Civic

Theatre. I also joined the Crucible Youth Theatre, even once appearing in Willy Russell's *Our Day Out* on the great stage itself. After a brief foray with the National Youth Theatre, I knew I'd found where I truly belonged. Even now, going into a theatre is the closest I get to any sort of spiritual experience. I adore old Victorian buildings, with their wonderful senses of history and mystery, and I've always said I would rather be a penniless actor than a rich anything else. Money can nourish my body but only acting can nourish my spirit.

I joined Saturday classes at the Rotherham College of Arts and Technology, where I'd enrol as a fulltime student at sixteen. I threw myself into courses covering mime, improvisation, role-playing and public speaking, as well as sidelines including lighting, make-up, creative writing and even kite making. If it was an aspect of performance, I wanted to immerse myself in it totally.

I took London Academy of Music and Dramatic Art (LAMDA) courses and certificates, and even gained their Silver Medal in spoken English. This was a close one though, as I nearly blew it for the first and only time in my life. I was petrified on stage, a bag of nerves, shaking and wringing my hands as the examiner chatted with me and asked questions. Fortunately, if there's one thing I excel at, it's homework! I'd done some background research on her previous work and favourite plays, so I steered the conversation toward those: 'Oh, that's one of my absolute favourites too! That staging was wonderful and helped inspire me to become an actor!' I passed with a distinction.

This was when I was happiest. In fact, these were the only times when I was anything even approaching happy. I attended every lesson I could, partly to absorb the information I craved, but mainly to avoid returning to the house. There was no happiness or comfort to be found there. The only silly scrap of consolation I held onto was an old blue and white pyjama case in the shape of a rabbit.

I was constantly plagued by migraines and nightmares. A recurring dream saw me in a forest, encountering an open, triple-walled building with no roof. The walls were high, white and sheer, and as I walked in a fourth wall closed behind me, trapping me in an open-air prison. I screamed for help as the walls came together but, even though I occasionally saw my father outside, no one ever came. Even at my age, it didn't take much to interpret this terrifying dream.

I'd named the pyjama case 'Rabbie', and he'd become something of a security blanket for me. There were many years of futile emotions tied up in him, mainly because they had no other outlet. One day my mother, for no apparent reason, went upstairs and snatched up this beloved creature. She made me watch as she sliced it to shreds with a large pair of scissors, all the time screaming I was a 'wooly woofter'. I first heard this loathsome phrase used on the Cannon and Ball prime time television show and, even then, was horrified it was permitted. I noticed she always laughed and took great delight in language like this and no doubt used it as a weapon. Years later, I was offered a pantomime with Cannon and Ball but had to turn it down. Even made in jest, such words could be confusing and hurtful, and so I couldn't bring myself to work with them. The destruction of Rabbie was pure spite with no other purpose than to wound me. It wasn't going to be her last such act.

2

PUT DOWN

The next year revealed some very unpleasant truths: some people actively hated me, and the rest just viewed me as an utterly irrelevant waste of skin. Three events in quick succession made it horribly apparent that I had nowhere to turn and no one to talk to.

My father was a pathetic creature, firmly under my aggressive mother's thumb, who must have had extra starch in his clothes as a substitute for his missing backbone. I wanted to be close to him, but he was so vapid and feeble that I think my pity would have turned to loathing if I had been. Coming from a poor background in Barnsley and marrying into a fairly well off family from Greece, he'd been downtrodden for years. I saw sadness in his eyes but there was never any chance of a bond between us. He seemed to accept his weakness and expected me to do the same with mine.

Unfortunately for him, we were completely different in that sense. He worked in his father-in-law's company, which was perhaps another reason for his lack of spirit as he was totally at the behest of the other side of his family. He was told what to do in his house and told what to do at his work.

I got the impression he was fairly able at his job, but otherwise he seemed dull witted, with no empathy or sympathy for anyone. Unless an opinion was officially sanctioned by his relatives, he wouldn't dream of considering it. I remember he joined a protest against a local chemicals plant that applied for a licence to process radioactive material. He was a NIMBY in the truest sense and found something where he was allowed to be vociferous, but with no understanding of the issue. I asked him why he didn't want the plant to do the work if it had been scientifically approved as safe, and why he was denying people jobs while his was perfectly secure. In return, I received the age-old answer parents morosely mutter when their spurious arguments are undermined: 'Shut up and go to your room. You're too young to understand.'

I'm afraid that couldn't have been further from the truth. He was just too stupid to understand, and dared not admit he was doing something to make it appear he wasn't a spineless weasel.

His cowardice and lack of love became blazingly clear when on a fateful night we headed out together to walk around another estate, posting leaflets for his company. Suddenly, three boys of thirteen years old jumped out in front and attacked me. They knocked me to the ground, landing punches and kicks with loud and joyous relish. I called out for my father's help, but he stood a few metres off, mutely watching. I seriously wondered if he actually enjoyed seeing this. The boys beat me, ripped my clothes off and, by the time they finished, I was half-naked, bleeding, and in floods of tears. They broke my nose and that injury is still apparent, as it remains out of alignment. I'd been kicked so hard repeatedly in the stomach that I was having difficulty breathing.

My father didn't say a word, just waited until I walked up to him. Without comment, he simply continued posting the leaflets. Some of the people in the houses around us must have witnessed what was happening, as there was enough shouting and screaming to rouse considerable attention. Again though, not one single person opened a door or uttered a word to break the hypocritical code of middle-class silence. Neither my mother, when we got back, nor any teacher the next day showed the remotest interest in my cuts, bruises or badly swollen eye. I was nine years old at the time.

From this point on, I no longer considered that I lived with my mother – just a vicious, cruel woman. There is no inherent reason why parents should like their children – or indeed vice versa – but there is a moral and legal requirement to care for them. She was only interested in inflicting pain, to try to compensate for her own perceived failures. I often wondered if she felt trapped by an expectation of playing a traditional housewife. She was in no way academically able and perhaps felt trapped and frustrated. Her response was to lash out and try to bring others down, seemingly in an attempt to make her feel less disappointed. I guess in that sense, I represented everything she aspired to and despised. This natural reaction to hate is something I've never understood from anyone.

Shortly afterwards, I was in art class and we were painting

Halloween scenes. There was one perpetually hostile boy in the group called Richard. At the end of the class, the teacher gave my painting to him and vice versa. I protested and she sniffed that my name should have been written on it. I turned the painting over to demonstrate that it was, but apparently her rule was that it had to be in pen, not pencil. I was merely to shut up and do as I was told.

I protested again and she swung around, grabbed the painting from my hand, ripped it up, slapped me across the face and sent me to detention. Even for someone for whom violence was becoming par for the course, this was outrageous.

Looking back, I now realise that Richard was probably ill and the staff were trying to protect him. Unfortunately, they ended up mollycoddling him and hurting everyone else. He was so desperate for attention that he continually got other children in trouble, as he knew the staff would do nothing to offend him.

One winter's night, Richard started throwing rocks and snowballs at me as I walked home alone. I bled, but I ignored him and trudged on. I hoped he got the message that his behaviour wasn't going to work with me, but the teachers were not quite so nuanced. They were unwilling to be honest and so they got it terribly wrong. I don't recall seeing Richard again and, although I have sympathy for what I imagine to be his situation, I certainly have none for the way he exploited it.

I don't pretend I was an angelic child, always perfectly behaved and pure of spirit – but then I've yet to meet one of those. The vicious, cruel woman took great joy in making me do things I disliked, including eating meat, despite my expressing a strong desire not to do so.

But the worst occasion came after the wedding of one of her friends. She forced me to wear a thick, blue cardigan of very coarse wool that itched terribly, even through my shirt. I sat in the church – an experience I certainly didn't relish in itself – and constantly scratched. At the reception, the bride asked me if I was okay. I hesitantly replied that I was fine, and the cardigan was just a bit uncomfortable. She suggested I take it off and, to her consternation, I innocently mentioned I wasn't allowed to.

Instantly, I realised the trouble I was in as I saw the woman glaring at me. Nothing could be allowed to sully her name in the eyes of others and, on arrival back at the house, she beat me with a long, wooden ruler. The onslaught was unrelenting and my begging her to stop fell on deaf ears. I started screaming for mercy, but this enraged her even more and she continued lashing at me for several minutes. I was cut, bruised, in extreme pain and utterly terrified. As ever, not one person the next day enquired as to what had happened. The teachers should have been ashamed of themselves, but of course they weren't. The truth was that they simply didn't care.

The final nail was hammered in while I was a member of the Cub Scouts. Someone's hat had gone missing, and the leader immediately accused me again. I assume the person responsible had given my name as a decoy, but rather than ask me if I'd taken it, I was accused and deprived of any opportunity to defend myself.

I was ordered outside in the dark to find the hat, despite

having no idea where it was. I found it after a long search and was then berated for wasting time. Naturally I was slapped again.

I graduated from the Cubs soon after and was expected to join the Boy Scouts. I surprised everyone when I declined, and the leaders took it as a personal affront. I was glad at this because it was certainly meant as one. The fact that they were simply incapable of understanding why was my main incentive.

Over the previous few months, my parents, teachers, scout leaders and others had all physically assaulted me. I had no refuge and no escape. But it was going to get much worse.

At eleven, I progressed to the local comprehensive school. I have never been in a place I've feared and despised more. I had no friends or confidants to help me through the next five years, and I can honestly say that the day in 1986 when I walked out of that building for the very last time was the happiest in my life. Some wonderful things have happened to me since, but no joy will ever be as all consuming.

Unfortunately, that wonderful time was still many years off. The three boys who'd previously attacked me on the estate were at the school, although I noted – with little surprise and an air of satisfaction – that they were in one of the lowest remedial classes. Nevertheless, after only a few months, they came at me again one day, completely unprovoked. It was in the playground at lunchtime, in broad daylight this time, and they were armed with cricket bats.

They hit me continually while the school's headmaster stood in a doorway and watched it all happen. I pleaded for him to do something, without response. When it mercifully ended, I stumbled over to him, but even to my jaded ear his answer was staggering. He told me there was nothing he could do if I wasn't bleeding, then turned his back and walked off. To have such a person supposedly caring for children was appalling. He tolerated bullying, violence and assault, and in my case at least, wouldn't lift a finger to prevent them. I swore there and then it would be the last time anyone laid a hand on me.

I didn't understand the headmaster at all. He was obviously very religious and kept trying to force his faith onto the children in assembly. I found this very unsettling, as in a secular school he was overstepping his authority and using his job to push a personal agenda. I clearly wasn't the only one who thought this way, as his efforts at indoctrination abruptly ceased and we weren't forced to listen to his private beliefs again. Mind you, we shouldn't have had to hear them in the first place.

As the next few years rolled by, my outlook on life and my individual prospects therein became ever bleaker. I just couldn't see the point if this was all there was – hardly a healthy view for a boy in his early teens.

But I was only a toddler when I'd worked out that religion was complete rubbish, and that there were no big answers to seek. Seriously, if anything as confusing and contradictory as religion were to be invented today, it'd be laughed out of existence. People only cling onto it in order to justify lifestyle choices that are usually prejudicial and self-serving. I'm a loving, tolerant person who lives my own life and, most importantly, takes responsibility for my own actions. Maybe I'm being naïve, but that seems a lot fairer and more grown-up to me.

But back in my schooldays, I was unloved and was frequently told so. I was ignored and hated by everyone – except one boy in my class called Justin. At thirteen I was among the tallest of the school's pupils, along with him, and then I suddenly stopped growing. I'd always imagined I'd be a statuesque adult of at least 190cm, but I annoyingly finished at 181cm. Evidently, even nature had it in for me!

Justin had no such problems and was easily the school's tallest by 14cm, but his brother, who was two years his junior, quickly overtook him and everyone else. Clearly, they have very lengthy genes in that particular pool!

Justin became a tentative friend and we regularly walked back at the end of the day together. We'd reach his house first, so I'd leave him there and continue alone. However, I'd go to walk for a few hours in the large woods behind the estate to avoid returning to the house where I lived. I was never in a rush to go back there.

(You'll notice I avoid using the word 'home' for the same reason I don't use 'family'. It just wasn't either.)

Justin and I talked, but I always wanted to open up to him. We both knew I was gay and, although he was happy and even keen to discuss it, I wasn't able to. I'd had it literally beaten into me that being gay was disgusting and wrong, that it made me a worthless piece of filth. I was clear-minded enough to recognise all this as lies, but I still couldn't quite break through.

For that, Justin, if you ever read this, I'm truly sorry. I so wanted to open up to you and trust you, but it would be a very long time until I achieved that with anyone.

The household I inhabited was very homophobic and

racist. There was a constant stream of derogatory terms used freely, usually by the woman. She also smoked and refused to let me leave the room, even though I was fully aware of what her poison was doing to me. The man, of course, would stay quiet and servile, but, just as he'd witnessed my assault in the street, perhaps he enjoyed my having to breathe the smoke.

Surely it can't be acceptable for adults to use 'queer', 'woofter', 'gypo', 'chink' and other such slurs in the presence of a child. If you want to be bigoted, that's up to your small mind but don't force those hatreds onto others – especially not impressionable minds for which you have some responsibility! This is why I'll never understand faith schools. Children are never sent to them for their own good, only because of the often arbitrarily chosen beliefs of their parents. That is forcing a lifestyle choice onto someone else, and I can never accept that as correct.

The environment made me so uneasy that, one day at dinner, I spoke up about some of the horrible language used. The woman jumped up, shouted at me and threw a cup of scalding coffee in my face. I screamed and instinctively pushed the glass table towards her, knocking her down. This was a moment of revelation for me, as I began to tentatively realise my strength of body as well as character. I turned and stared at the man, daring him to try and stop me while she lay shocked on the floor.

In intense pain, I stormed out of the house, slamming the door so hard the glass in the lower panel shattered. I had just turned sixteen and was certain I had to make ready to leave there permanently. I had never been so furious before and was visibly shaking with adrenalin. I was actually scared of the consequences it might lead to.

I had a younger sister. She took after the woman and, as she grew older, the similarities became more pronounced. Neither was intelligent, so they liked to put other people down in order to make themselves feel less wretched. I tried to communicate with Jill but such efforts were doomed to failure. One Sunday, the woman was watching us fold laundry and told me that if there was any kind of disagreement, she would always believe the girl's word over mine and reminded me I would never be trusted.

I turned to my sibling and asked how she could allow her to speak like that. I received a chilling echo in response: 'Who's she? The cat's mother?' This idiotic answer was a favourite phrase of the woman, who always demanded to be addressed respectfully. An English teacher had once demanded this of me when I said, 'What?' instead of 'Pardon?', and I offered the opinion that surely respect should be earned rather than expected. She wasn't happy and made me leave the room. As always, the automatic reaction of those with too little intelligence to reason is to be angry or dismissive.

After the girl uttered those words, it was clear she'd made her choice of how she wanted to live. I immediately and permanently lost all respect for her, and would make no further attempts to bond. If even the person nominally closest to me lacked the brains or the stomach to stand up, I'd much rather be alone. Such stupidity and cowardice sickened me, but based on everything I'd seen until that point, it seemed that was the way people were. Those with the least to say invariably shout loudest in the hope of drowning out everyone else.

I didn't go back to the house that night, and slept instead in the relative warmth of the town-centre bus station. It was a large concrete edifice built just after the war. The thick, featureless walls retained heat and offered shadow, so a bench tucked away at the back might avoid too much attention. I looked up to the line of small windows high above me, slightly below the level of the roof, and became conscious of my personal nightmare.

That was my initiation to sleeping rough, and I thanked my luck for the relative ease with which it passed. I missed school the next day, but when I returned it was a casual clothing day. Everyone was wearing their own outfits rather than the stark school uniform. As the solitary person in black trousers, blazer and tie, I was rather surprised and relieved that none of my classmates commented on it.

Even though the teachers were expert at turning blind eyes, my black ones were all too obvious to the other children. They knew what was going on, but of course they were powerless. Perhaps they at least silently sympathised, even if they didn't reach out. But beneath my hardening exterior I still wished that they would, as I was desperate for someone to talk to.

For here was a young man, still essentially a child, with the certainty that he was entirely alone: he'd only ever had one friend; his parents had physically and verbally attacked him all his life; he'd been assaulted by a gang with bats while uncaring eyes looked on; and he'd endured years of abuse and been told to his face that he was worthless and would be better off dead.

Nobody could ever stand by and let that happen, could they? But many people did for fear of getting involved, or of being attacked or accused themselves. I understand those reasons but can't possibly ever accept them. They hardly excuse those who didn't care, or the continuing indifference every time that the boy I was showed up bleeding or bruised.

Sorry for getting philosophical here, but there's a poignant quotation by Edmund Burke I'm often reminded of: 'The only thing necessary for the triumph of evil is for good men to do nothing.'

The people ignoring the abuse were as complicit as those committing it. Quite possibly, they'd have been happier if the young man had just died. Hey presto, the problem solved itself!

I'd wanted my life to end before it had really begun. Only two years later, I would try to make that a reality.

A respectable, middle-class façade is no assurance of tranquillity within. I tried reporting what was happening to teachers and neighbours but was met with disinterest or disbelief. As a last resort, I even went to the local police station. I stood alone in the unwelcoming foyer and waited to be summoned forwards. The blonde woman attending the desk looked up and, with no level of politeness or professionalism, gestured with a snort that I should approach.

I explained why I was there but had hardly started when she literally laughed in my face. She dismissively told me to go and tell my teachers, waving her hand and expecting me to leave. When I insisted I'd already tried that, she looked down her nose and sneered, with a condescending chuckle, 'Well, who are we supposed to believe then?'

I pleaded with her to listen, but she turned her back and began chatting breezily with her colleagues. In the light of recent revelations about the South Yorkshire police service, I'm no longer as surprised by this attitude. They forgot they were paid public servants, and that a child crying out for help should never be told to get lost. It seems they acted in the same way on many more occasions.

*   *   *

I sat my exams at school and qualified in the top group with nine O-level passes. I urgently hoped my experience of school was now over but had to endure the tedious convention of the presentation ceremony. Each student was called forward and given a certificate by the headmaster. As one of the top dozen, I was called up very early.

I walked deliberately slowly to the stage and the headmaster congratulated me. I was a lead actor in the dramatic society and the school chess champion, so he commented that he'd be happy to write a reference with a dramatic slant to it. He reached out his hand to shake mine but I remained stoic. I replied quietly, barely concealing my rage at his callous stupidity, saying I'd refuse anything from someone who approved of children in his care being attacked while he watched. I left his waiting hand suspended in mid air as I took my certificate and walked off stage. Now, I really wish I'd shouted it for the whole hall to hear, but at the time I was so happy with my first defiant fight-back against an oppressive system. I walked down to return to my seat. I noticed the shocked faces of the complicit teachers and ignorant parents but also the faint approving smiles of some of the children. By then though, I was well past seeking, or caring about, their acceptance.

Back at the house nothing was said, as the woman was clearly very apprehensive of me now. I was a strong, fit young man and I doubt she wanted to tip me further over the edge. Believe me, it wouldn't have taken much. I yearned to hurt them both for the way they had treated me, but, having endured their hatred and intolerance from an early age, I was determined to be better than they were.

On reading this back, I've depicted myself as a cold, bitter teenager, but that's the inescapable truth. Be candid with yourself: if you'd been in my position, how might you have turned out? I'm fortunate that the saving grace of my life would help mould me to be the person I am today. That time was still more than a decade away though, and things were going to get a lot darker before then.

Within the next six months, my life would change beyond all recognition. Although I had no way of realising it then, ultimately it would all be for the best. The old adage about having to hit rock bottom before rising up would prove terrifyingly accurate.

I gratefully left school and entered college to study English and Performance Arts. The theatre was where I needed to be, so I immersed myself in its world. With my difficulty in making friends, however, the inevitable cliques formed quickly without me. Maybe it's just us artistic types (although I can't see it personally), but the daily dialogues appeared to be each group bitching about each other. The only signs of teamwork were when they joined forces to turn on any outsiders.

However, after a few weeks, my academic and theatrical abilities gained a sort of uneasy respect and I began to settle. Then, shortly afterwards, I faced the greatest upheaval of my life so far – I fell in love.

He was a fellow student called Mark, who was very uncomfortable with his sexuality. But still we began a tentative relationship, culminating in my first kiss. We crept into a locked park after college one evening and sat down on a bench, just looking at each other. After a few moments we kissed, and I was wrapped in total bliss. I tried to cling onto that feeling during what immediately followed.

I arrived at college the next day to find my locker smashed in and 'fuck off' written on the door. I reported this to the college head but was quickly waved away with the head commenting that I was wrong to be involved in such practices. Clearly, ignoring an uneasy situation was more important than protecting students, or even college property. I do wonder if this is a general approach taken by teaching staff. Have they really forgotten how it was to be young, puzzled and seeking guidance?

We are all human beings, and our needs, desires and problems are pretty much universal. Of course, it's different now in the age of the internet, but I'm still shocked by the statistics showing how few parents talk to their children about sex. The most natural and pleasurable of human activities is stigmatised, bizarrely, as the most shameful.

What a load of rubbish! I'm so lucky now that I have friends who, like me, lack inhibitions, so that no subjects are off limits. It saddens me terribly when I read about young people who die needlessly because they're too afraid to discuss a medical problem. We should be celebrating our differences, not nervously pretending they don't exist or don't matter. But rather than being open and frank, we prefer to suffer in embarrassed silence. I did that for years, and I'm damned if I will again.

* * *

My circumstances in and out of college continued deteriorating. In early 1987, they became intolerable. In the middle of March, my parents booked me in to see a psychiatrist. I may have been clinically depressed but, of course, the fault was entirely mine as no one else was willing to admit to any culpability.

I spoke as calmly as I could and explained everything over two hours. I explained how torrid my school life had been and slowly built up to more personal subjects. He offered very few responses, forcing me to continue talking to fill the uncomfortable silences. Although I'd vaguely hinted at it with a couple of people at college, he was the first person I'd opened up to, even at a tentative level. I told him how my parents had abused, threatened and assaulted me. I tried to make him understand what I'd gone through for the past decade and a half and how there seemed to be no escape for me. He nodded and I began to hope I'd found someone who'd be willing to offer me an olive branch.

He listened attentively for nearly two hours until I was thoroughly drained but I couldn't help noticing he'd hardly written a thing down. When I'd finished he looked directly at me and, in a condescending tone, told me through thinly smiling lips that I was a liar. I'd made the whole thing up for attention.

I'm not sure how I resisted hitting him, as I'd never felt such an urge to lash out at someone. I stood up while he was still talking and walked out. But I accepted by now that adults believed they could treat me like this with impunity, so why shouldn't they? Who was going to stop them? Yet again, my honesty had met with the standard withering response. He called in my parents, but I knew exactly how the conversation was going to go. I walked off and didn't return to the house until many hours later when the predictable happened.

The woman began ranting with increasing volume and ferocity about how nasty and manipulative I was.

'How could you say that to him?' she shouted, further confirming my belief that she didn't care what she did, she only cared about other people finding out. 'All you want to do is cause problems for us. We should have put you into care long ago, but it's too late now so just piss off. It'd all be better if you were dead.'

That was all I needed. I snapped and screamed in fury at the top of my voice. Despite she and her wimp husband frantically resisting from the other side, I forced the kitchen door open and stood directly in front of her. She was terrified but, after a decade and a half of feeling exactly the same, I had absolutely no sympathy and maliciously relished the fear etched on her face. I stood still, daring this horrible, abusive bully to move before I turned away in satisfaction and disgust.

It was a few days later and not one word had been uttered between us in the meantime. The man came to talk to me. He tried to be conciliatory, but he was blaming me for everything and asking why couldn't I be a good little boy? At that point, he should have been grateful that I abhor violence, because otherwise I wouldn't have restrained myself. Instead, I called him a spineless drip and left.

But I don't just mean I left the room; I left the house, and this time it was for good. I wanted to be free of these sick tormentors forever, and the price I paid was immaterial.

It was 23 March 1987. In only a pair of jeans, a t-shirt and shoes, I walked out into a torrential rainstorm. I knew a student named Michael from college, who was in the year above me; we'd chatted a few times and, having been to his house, I just about remembered where lived. Unfortunately, it was fifteen miles away, but I had no choice but to begin my cold, soaking journey. I felt none of it, however, as I was too overcome with sheer relief.

I arrived about nine in the evening. With no money to call, in an era before mobile phones, Michael was surprised to see this bedraggled figure standing in his doorway. He ushered me in at once and I related the evening's events. I was so upset as I sat there in front of the open fireplace, trying to dry my drenched clothes as they adhered to my body. I finally accepted he was trying to help when he insisted I get changed, and offered me a bathrobe to wear instead.

The next day we went to see his friend Liam. Even though he was straight, Liam had somehow become the college's unofficial counsellor for young people coming out as gay. At the time, I inwardly smiled at such a benign notion, but this later turned to annoyance when the truth dawned on me. He'd been given the responsibility because none of the staff wanted it, or were even prepared to admit it was necessary.

I stayed with him for a night and he then found me a bed at a hostel – overlooking the spot where Mark and I shared that kiss. I lasted precisely two nights in that place. We weren't allowed to watch television unless it was what the volunteers wanted, and there was an incredible notice listing forbidden topics of discussion, including homosexuality.

Forbidden topics? It was 1987, not an Orwellian 1984! Bear in mind though that the age of consent for gay people then was still twenty-one, and appalling legislation like Section 28 was being enacted. It was hardly a conducive environment for a vulnerable gay man to grow up in. Talking was precisely what I needed to do, and here was a place ostensibly providing shelter but flatly denying help.

I sincerely hope that, in my experience as a volunteer, I've never been so rude to or dismissive of people asking for my compassion. I've never believed that the capacity to love is a character defect or a sign of weakness. I'm so glad that neither myself nor those closest to me now are afraid to let down those social barriers. Not only can we see from behind our twitching curtains, we'll talk openly about it too.

So, in late March 1987, I pulled the anorak I'd been given around me and headed towards the park once more. I climbed over the locked gate and looked for a bench, but specifically avoided that special one. I lay down and closed my eyes but managed less than an hour's sleep as I was cold, terrified and painfully aware of being totally alone. I lacked money or any idea of how I was going to live or eat.

The human spirit can be powerful though, and I'm

fortunate to be really bloody-minded. Somehow I knew I'd be able to last a few days until I got out of this mess. I'd escaped those sadists and was finally taking back my own life. Yes, it'd been a rocky start, what with sleeping rough, but if that was the price I had to pay, it was surely worth it.

But if I'd known then that I'd still be on the streets nearly three years later, would I have made the same choices? The answer is invariably, 'Hell, yes!'

Let me lay one thing out for you right now. I rarely look back as I don't see the point. If it's happened, it can't be changed so let it go and get on with life, that's my motto. For many people, this isn't an option, but if they want to bring you down, just think about that for a moment. If they're intent on dragging you down, they're already down there and you're above them. You should never look down on people unless you're helping them up.

I can't describe how I felt about those in my past. Even now, I refuse to use the word 'hate' in conversation or on social media as it's simply too negative. Don't misunderstand me. I neither pity nor will ever forgive them, as they knew perfectly well what they were doing. They're just unimportant, as I accept full responsibility for my own life and make no excuses for my choices or mistakes. If you don't like where you are, you can leave and that's exactly what I did.

Of course we've all made decisions that turned out badly, but I've never regretted a single one of mine. Good or bad, the road taken was the right one at the time, so why fret about an event you can't change? That's the very definition of futility, and regret is rather like hate. You get nothing from hanging onto something so distracting and self-destructive. Just let it go and be free.

And for the first time in my life, I truly was.

3

ESCAPE TO NOWHERE

My freedom had come at considerable cost. Don't get me wrong – it was absolutely the right thing to do and the only practical decision I could make, but I was now utterly isolated. I knew no one would ever make any effort to look for or contact me, and nearly three decades later I'm yet to be proven incorrect. I was at a complete loss as to what to do or where to go now.

I returned to the bus station and to the imagery of my chilling dream. It's strange how certain places can reawaken long-forgotten memories, but I could now appreciate how this building wasn't my prison but my way out.

I slept in the same discreet corner for two more nights, but thought better of it after a student from college saw me one evening. He came up and just spat at me, snarling that I'd let him and others down by not coming into class. I weakly tried to explain my reasons but he didn't listen, and besides – all the strength and fight had drained out of me.

My most pressing dilemma was how to find something to eat. Drinking water was plentiful in public toilets and facilities, but food was rather scarcer. In the following years, I'd become a very strict vegetarian as I'd been keen to pursue this path since I was about six. But in my current predicament I was prepared to be a little less fastidious.

I've never drank alcohol in my life – literally never even taken a sip of it – and that's the way it'll always stay. I've seen what it can do to people, even at low levels, and I won't allow that to happen to me. I refuse to lose control of my body and mind, however temporarily, and fail to see the attraction of staggering around a town centre in the small hours being violently sick. Perhaps it's the pinnacle of a great night out for some people, but I'm afraid the appeal is lost on me and I find the smell of alcoholic drinks quite repulsive. I don't need to go near the stuff to be sure I won't like it, so the temptation is never there

One common tragedy that affects many homeless people is sheer hopelessness. Drinking may be just a superficial patch, but then the pattern is very difficult to break. Despair takes over and is exacerbated by what often becomes uncontrollable alcoholism. It's a spiral that ends in just a few likely outcomes.

Despite my problems, I was fortunate in being both intelligent and practical. I sincerely believed I deserved something better, and wanted to stick around long enough to discover what it was. I had a glimmer of hope to hang onto, but I recognise that it put me in a very fortunate minority.

One thing I held onto from my five months at college was a passage from the book *Schindler's Ark*, later adapted into the Oscar-winning film *Schindler's List*. There was a very distressing scene where a pair of women are led off to what they think is a gas chamber. One decides to kill herself before reaching it in order to deny their captors the satisfaction. The other implores her to refrain from suicide, otherwise she'll never truly know what the outcome would have been. I kept that sentiment very close to my heart and it helped me through some of the struggles ahead.

Although I wasn't bereft of hope, I lacked purpose. What was I supposed to do to occupy myself during the daytime? I had nowhere to go for those seemingly endless hours when my sole aim was to stay alive.

I gladly lost myself in the public library, where it was at least warm and quiet. There were toilets where I could wash myself, and books to help me forget my reality, however briefly. I tried to gain some sort of social security via the benefits office, but the queues were interminable and I always seemed to get a counter assistant in a bad mood.

After a few visits I was offered temporary accommodation in an adult hostel, but the woman attending to me said that honestly, off the record, I'd be better off fending for myself on the streets. The place was deliberately designed to be unappealing, often with ten or more residents to each room. Violence was common and she couldn't in good conscience recommend it to a vulnerable person like me. I got the distinct impression she believed it to be the very least that could be offered by the council, while paying lip service to unenthusiastic government targets. The fewer people who stayed there, the less cost would be incurred. Therefore, the experience was set up to be as off-putting as possible.

Being seventeen, I was to be processed as an adult, even though other aspects of the law didn't recognise me as such. I asked about money, but the application process was convoluted and generally only accepted when the applicant had a permanent address. I lacked even the ability to prove my identity, as I had no documents with me, so the system was made virtually inaccessible. My options were presented starkly: either remain homeless or move to a hostel with a less-than-£20-a-week allowance that would probably get stolen from me anyway.

The food issue was getting ever more desperate, and this led to a few months that I gravely wished I could have avoided. I daren't yet bring myself to beg, especially not in the town where I grew up; someone was bound to see me or I'd end up arrested, assaulted or worse, so I had no option but to resort to stealing food. I'm not proud of this but neither do I regret it. I simply did what was essential.

In the last few years I've thrown myself into charity work. I'd be so much better off financially if it wasn't for my liberal guilt! But back then, every dubious act I committed was because I was unable to see an alternative. I hope I've more than made up for these transgressions since, but unless you've experienced such anxiety personally, it's impossible to know how deep the chasm goes. I'll unashamedly say that, if I had to, I'd do it all over without a moment's hesitation.

I had to strike some sort of balance, if only to prevent my moral compass from whirring out of control. So I ruled out stealing from individuals; appearances can be deceptive, so there would be no certainty that they were able to afford it. Naturally then, I preferred larger shops or supermarkets, accepting the downside that security increased the chances of being caught.

I only took the minimum I needed to feed myself, and with experience gained a considerable degree of skill. One time in Marks and Spencer, I indicated to the staff another shoplifter and strolled out of the store as they detained him. No time for honour amongst thieves here; the fact that he was tucking a bottle of Baileys into his bag allowed me to rationalise my crime over his. I discovered a newfound pride at my level of shoplifting proficiency, albeit tinged with a growing alarm. I'm sure I'd have made a very successful career criminal had I been so inclined.

I knew I needed to get out of Rotherham before I could reasonably expect to make a fresh start, so I hitchhiked to the seaside town of Skegness. I continued my petty theft but knocked it down to a single item a day. There was a butcher's on the high street that sold trays of four or five blocks of cheese. These were quite easy to slip inside my jacket and kept me sustained for a few weeks. I slept on a bench on the seafront, as it was a warm summer and blissfully dry.

One early morning I woke to find someone had left a few coins by me. I walked back to the butcher's and bought a cheese tray. The staff behind the counter looked at me in disbelief – it was immediately evident they knew what I'd been up to every day. They'd been letting me get away with it out of sympathy for my obvious situation. I was so overcome with remorse and gratitude, I never stepped foot inside that shop again. I don't know if the place is still there, but if so, thank you all.

Around the end of July, I left Skegness and made my way to Sheffield. This was the big city within my personal sphere, as it lay a mere ten miles from Rotherham. I continued with my life of expedient crime but was getting increasingly uncomfortable with how naturally it now came to me.

There was a big roundabout in Sheffield centre that used to have a large open air hole in it. Below this was an underpass and several crisscrossing subway tunnels, and I slept huddled in these. Before too long, the nights began to close in, the temperature dropped and I had to leave. I could easily deal with all the people walking by, studiously ignoring me, as it was exactly the reaction I wanted. To be honest, I'd have been mortified if anyone had come up to or spoken to me.

I instinctively shunned all human contact and cut a sorry, filthy figure, wearing the same clothes I'd had on for four months. They were visibly falling apart, but one day I saw a Salvation Army van parking and decided to chance my arm. I spoke to the driver, who turned out to be a volunteer called Charlie. He offered to take me to the outreach and broke the rules by giving me a hot drink, a couple of new things to wear and, most importantly, a decent pair of second-hand shoes. He took pity on me at that point and would try to help whenever he could.

It was during my stay in Sheffield that I visited my first gay bar. The Cossack was an old, rather traditionally-styled pub that had been the centre of the city's small gay scene for many years. Charlie, who was in his mid-thirties, took me in one Friday. I was hardly the most attractive person on show as a constant diet of stolen cheese was hardly great for my complexion. Nevertheless, I was happy not to leave the pub alone that evening – though the man I left with, who was about twenty-three, was technically guilty of child rape. That's how ridiculous the law was at the time.

The prospect of bed hopping hardly appealed as a long-term solution, so I had to make up my mind concerning my immediate future. Any dreams about a life on the stage had been firmly discarded; my only priority was making it from one day to the next.

The following Monday, I arrived as the Salvation Army opened its doors for one final call. I cleaned up as best I could, embraced Charlie and walked the few miles to the M1. I stuck out my thumb and waited for a lift to London. I had no clear plan of what to do once I got to the capital but intuitively believed it was for the best. A clean break meant a clean slate, so where better to begin the story anew than hidden in plain sight among the faceless bustle of millions?

During those last years of the Thatcher government, London was undergoing a draconian facelift intended to remove the homeless from the streets. I agree that the ends were justifiable but the means employed were most certainly not. I was dropped slap bang in the middle of it and witnessed it from the opposite viewpoint.

We only get through our daily lives by blinkering ourselves against the harsh realities of the world. Would we be able to function if we concentrated on the wars, famines, diseases and other horrors that constantly afflict our fellow humans? We're not blind or uncaring about them but have to employ selective vision. In Britain, we give very generously to charity and this assuages our guilt. We're happy to put a hand in our pocket as long as it guarantees insulation from what's really going on. That's laudable, but it's very different for those on the other side, especially so when it's close to home.

By Waterloo station was the now-infamous Cardboard City. As a new arrival, this was where I naturally gravitated. I'd heard the reputation of the place, but hoped I could find some camaraderie with those in the same situation. I was disabused of such wishful thinking with shocking alacrity.

No words can paint a genuine picture of what that place was like. It was an offence to all the senses and remains vivid in my mind after all these years. Hundreds of people packed together under bridges, in subways and in doorways, a mass of dirty, fraught humanity suffering the indignity of abandonment. The stench was unimaginable, even in the open air, but worse than everything else was a perceptible sense of menace born of despair. It bubbled under the surface and was destined to blow at some point. Mute souls gathered around braziers to keep warm but apart from a few groups of all age ranges, most opted for solitude. There was always the unspoken threat of violence, and nobody wanted to be conspicuous enough to set it off.

I fully understand the authorities' desire to clean this festering sore and sanitise the whole area. I was dismayed by how scared and resentful the daily commuters were. It was a mainly nocturnal gathering, but every day a large crowd of rail, tube and bus travellers made its way back and forth. It must have come into close contact with this cesspit, and I pictured each eyeing the other with suspicion.

Within a few hours of discovering this awful limbo, I had

my shoes and jacket forcibly taken from me. I accept now that this was no particularly malevolent act, merely survival of the fittest. In my state of malaise, it was a battle I was always going to lose.

I can't vouch for its accuracy, but I heard a story that circulated about a man arrested after causing an affray in central London. He'd been sleeping rough for a short time but was already in an extremely bad way, and very emaciated. Unusually, he was well-spoken and superbly educated but died soon afterwards, having previously stated to anyone who enquired that he no longer wanted to live. Apparently, until a matter of weeks before, he'd been the CEO of a major company. But one morning, he was backing his car out of his garage and ran over his wife and son. From that moment on, his life was effectively over.

This story, whether true or not, has always stayed like a splinter in my consciousness. We're all only a couple of pay cheques or one tragic moment away from oblivion. It's only a shared mass delusion that keeps us all teetering along the knife edge.

*　　*　　*

It was December and I was spending my first full day in London on the streets with a pair of jeans, underpants, socks and a long sleeved t-shirt to my name. It was a matter of some urgency to find warm clothes and food, so I asked a few people if there was a hostel or shelter nearby. Most ignored me or didn't know but eventually a lovely older chap directed me to a centre only a minute's walk away. I went in and silently waited in the corridor until early afternoon, when someone was available to see me.

The staff members were earnestly polite, but I suppose they'd seen it all before. The only way to handle it in certain professions is to remain utterly aloof. You hear stories of morgue workers joking brazenly about death and corpses; this might appear terribly inappropriate, but just seems an obvious method of getting on with a morbid job. I don't think the majority of their clients would be bothered, after all.

But emotional detachment didn't make it any easier to this poor sod who needed help and a sensitive ear. I was mildly berated for not having made an appointment, and I reluctantly bit my lip, sitting there shoeless and shivering. The beds were off limits, as I'd have to claim housing benefit. I'd been through this rigmarole before and was well aware of how futile it could be. I agreed to try the next morning, expecting they'd let me stay the night but no such offer was forthcoming. I tried in vain to explain the confounding paradox they were unwilling to see beyond: I wasn't permitted to stay at that address until I'd claimed the appropriate benefits, but, conversely, was denied the right to claim said benefits without the address.

Until someone took the first step toward trusting me and issued some identification, I was stuck between a rock and a hardheaded place. My reward was the typical officious blank stare of those charged with enforcing petty rules uncomprehendingly, the very definition of the term 'jobsworth'. Ironically, a few weeks earlier I would have qualified for immediate help as, legally, I was still a child. But as I'd now passed my eighteenth birthday, I was expected to navigate up a certain creek without the necessary means of propulsion.

I asked if they could at least help with some clothes and shoes. That particular spark of human decency hadn't been extinguished, or perhaps they just had an officially approved course of action they could now follow. They gave me completely fresh clothing, extra socks, underwear and a lovely warm overcoat. I promised myself this coat would be staying with me, and me alone. A small shoulder bag to carry my humble possessions topped me off.

Then came an unexpected treat. I was offered a haircut, as the visiting barber was at the centre that day. It's those moments of sudden unanticipated joy that can make such a difference, and I gratefully accepted, as it'd been nine months since my last. I asked for it to be cut very short, as I didn't know when I'd next get the chance. The barber kindly cautioned against this, as the cold weather would make me grateful for anything covering my head. I gladly agreed and thanked him for his sage advice.

Perhaps the staff felt a little guilty about not helping more, as they directed me into a private bathroom where I enjoyed a long and blisteringly-hot shower. I didn't mind the awful-smelling soap, as the water scalding off months of dirt and grease was so pleasurable. I was even able to brush my teeth, an event conspicuous by its rarity that year. It's these little, banal things I'd missed the most. We all enjoy and settle into our soothing routines and even the slightest variance can be jarring. I'd had a cataclysmic upheaval, and feeling a dreary toothbrush between my fingers was like an epiphany.

Finally, I was invited to join the residents for the evening meal, but when I saw the same sorts of faces I'd seen in Cardboard City I became apprehensive and made my excuses. A makeshift cup of soup was provided, a couple of chocolate bars stuffed into my bag and I was led outside. It was about 5pm and dark, but within moments I hit the bright lights of Trafalgar Square and a sea of bodies, the like of which I'd never witnessed before. I gawped and took it all in, and it suddenly dawned on me: I wasn't cold. I savoured this relief with delight, trying not to think of the long night ahead.

I wanted to sleep somewhere quiet, but should I run the risk of violence in a secluded place? Having nobody else around might put me in a potentially dangerous situation. I also reasoned that the more remote the location, the greater the chance of it being inhospitably cold. I decided to try my luck on the Strand, so I walked up and down a few times looking for a suitable position. With my new attire, no one gave me a second glance and I gladly melted into the sea of unseeing eyes. As I wasn't very tired and it was likely to be many hours before the road quietened down, I decided to walk and get to know the area.

I wandered down to Aldwych, up to Holborn and across to Tottenham Court Road. I suddenly found myself at the eastern end of Oxford Street and harked back to being here once before, as a six-year-old. With no objective, I set off into the commotion of the world's busiest shopping thoroughfare. Bright lights, deafening noise and the unending movement of traffic and people all conspired to make me feel very small indeed. I rapidly grew depressed as I travelled further, and even started looking into the faces of my fellow pedestrians for a comforting smile or nod of acknowledgement. Unsurprisingly, I saw neither, as London is hardly a haven for strangers and what little seasonal spirit there was had been firmly trampled underfoot in the spending frenzy.

I reached Oxford Circus and looked ahead into a horde that appeared even more impenetrable than the one I'd just made my way through. I looked for an immediate escape route but Regent Street offered no respite, so I cut down behind the tube station and saw a sight that immediately evoked my previous visit from a dozen years ago. Shining before me was the legendary London Palladium.

I stood staring at the white façade, transfixed for several minutes. I'd been here to see Michael Crawford in *Barnum*, and although I remember his tightrope walk, I can't recall anything else from the show sadly. I was aware of the crowds pushing around me, but it seemed no more than a dream as I took in each tiny detail of the theatre's perfection. Here once more, I was thunderstruck by an almost spiritual connection to a place I hardly knew. Of course, it was never going to come to fruition, but here I was, certain to my very core that I was an actor.

I continued on through Carnaby Street to Soho, eventually arriving at Old Compton Street. I'd been told that this, along with Earl's Court, was the main gay village of London. I stopped in the middle of the road, dumbfounded, as I'd never seen anything like it. Guys were drinking with each other, holding hands and even kissing in full view of the street, and not one person walking past gave a damn. I was still three years below the legal age of consent, but peering in the windows, like a kid in a candy store, it was obvious that I wasn't the only one.

This is how it should be, I thought: live and let live! I smiled to myself, but was instantly upset that I didn't have any money to go in and buy a drink. More than anything at that moment, I wanted to absorb the atmosphere of this cosmopolitan paradise. I belonged here; these were literally my people, but I was denied the chance to join them. This was the moment I decided there was nothing else for it – I was going to have to beg.

Of course, I had no concept of how to proceed with my new venture but guessed a high, regular footfall would provide the best chance. After all, it wasn't as if I needed that much cash; a few pounds would easily see me through the evening. Surely such a meagre ambition wouldn't be too difficult or time-consuming to fulfil.

I wound my way back to the Strand and headed for Charing Cross station. I caught a glance of myself in a window and was shocked as, for a change, I looked nothing like a traditional beggar. I removed my coat, found a dry spot inside one of the corridors leading to the station forecourt, carefully folded it up and sat on it. At least I could rely on genuine shivers to tug those heartstrings now.

I considered youth to be my main advantage, as hopefully this might gain a little sympathy. I couldn't have been more wrong, as an hour later I was no better off. I wasn't prepared to hassle anyone, and instead limited myself to the occasional mumbled request for spare change. Maybe I was unlucky and all the commuters had holiday tunnel vision, but they resolutely refused to look. I was getting ready to give up when two policemen walked up and stood over me.

I shan't go into specifics concerning their language, but I've never used such words even when alone and wouldn't want to be associated with anyone who did. They mocked my obvious distress and called me worthless filth, littering their speech with expletives they clearly thought were not only acceptable but also completely appropriate. I picked up my bag and coat and slinked off as they laughed at my back.

These tactics became more overt soon after, when Cardboard City was very aggressively cleansed. This was no subtle or compassionate process; human beings who had nothing but a few vestiges of dignity were stripped of even that. Clothes, shelters and possessions were all burnt, and these sad figures removed by force. Yes, the whole community – if I can call it that – was a terrible blight on the face of one of the world's great cities. This, however, was no solution, and zero kindness was shown to the displaced. Not a single thought was given to where they were supposed to go. Families, children and babies were unceremoniously dumped over a few short days. I shudder to think how many survived but remain unconvinced that it was very many.

I tried a couple of other places but sleep was never easy to come by, as the police or shop owners frequently moved me on. Anonymous feet kicked me, either by accident or intentionally, and I was targeted by drunkards, abusive passersby and drug pushers. Despite this, I'm grateful that I was never seriously physically assaulted in all of my time sleeping rough. It's ironic, then, that on the two occasions I was badly beaten up, my father and headmaster, who were nominally supposed to protect me, had watched it all. I was definitely better off here.

I was occasionally given a few coins, usually dropped while I was asleep. It appeared that even such scarce acts of kindness had to be done out of sight. A local supermarket provided sustenance, but this was usually just dry bread and chocolate, hardly a lasting option.

Christmas Day popped up, but I was disheartened not to see one charity worker. I'd expectantly looked forward to this day, thinking I'd at least get a warm bed and some food, but no advances were made. I walked around the unsettlingly quiet streets looking for a soup kitchen, but found none. I'm sure there must have been one, but if those in need didn't know where it was, then why bother? As I've said, not everyone in need is able to access services so it has to be a two-way street.

This is why, remembering how lonely I was in 1987, I never let that day pass without a little effort. Every 25th of December, I go out with bags full of food, water and warm socks to hand out to any homeless people I see. I've repeatedly tried to volunteer with charities but virtually all insist on a minimum commitment. This is another example of bureaucracy blocking its own purpose, so I prefer to get off my backside and do it myself. All the years I've gone out, I've still failed to spot a charity van or worker anywhere.

Every person I've met on these forays has been gracious. The supplies on offer have been politely taken or declined. One lady, though, reminded me horribly of the story of the CEO. She was sitting all alone behind the Covent Garden Opera House, wrapped in a flimsy blanket. She had a bottle of whisky in her hand and smelled as if it had been her exclusive diet for a while. I asked if she'd like a sandwich or some chocolate, but, without any sadness, she bluntly said no, as she was just waiting to die.

I tried to nod and to speak, but what possible response is there to that? I turned away and began sobbing uncontrollably at what had brought this poor lady to say such a thing here, in one of the world's richest cities, in the twenty-first century. Care of its citizenry should be the primary responsibility of any government, but unless the system changes, these people will forever slip, unnoticed, onto the lowest rung.

As I discovered when I tried to claim benefits, if you have no address, you're not on the electoral register, so neither you nor your vote count. Unfortunately, my little trips are no longer limited to one day a year, as the need is always with us. Believe me, a bite of food and a kind word goes much further than you can imagine to someone unused to either.

Back on the cusp of 1988, there came the habitual holiday sales. The city centre was ludicrously overstuffed with angry people, competing against each other to see who could carry the most shopping bags. The prospect of staying put during this unbridled terror wasn't appealing, so I extracted myself from the melee and relocated to the South Bank. I thought this might provide an oasis of calm as there were relatively few cafes or shops. I did, however, squirm when it struck me how close I was to Waterloo and the neighbourhood of which I'd briefly been a part.

An idea had been rattling around in my skull for some time and was getting increasingly difficult to blank out. I tried to ignore it and to cling onto the foolish notion that something else, anything else, would turn up. I'd tormented myself for weeks but, as the cold nights had grown ever more punishing, my list of realistic alternatives diminished. This was a step I didn't want to take, but I was in real danger of freezing or starving to death. That may sound melodramatic, but put yourself in my position: would you clutch at any straw for a chance to live? I was definitely stubborn enough, so my head ultimately overruled my heart.

Necessity is indeed the mother of invention, and this was a potential resolution to my impending crisis, despite all my heartfelt resistance. It was New Year's Eve and I reasoned that if anything was going to come of it, today might represent the perfect timing. The demand might be higher and the supply lower, so perhaps I stood a decent chance of having my services accepted. I knew of an address in South Kensington, so I made my way there and knocked on the door of a basement flat.

After a brief meeting with the Thai owner, I was welcomed in. I showered, shaved and sat down nervously in a small room with four other young men. I tried to look relaxed, but my feeling was one of defeated depression and my stomach churned. I was now waiting for my first client as a male prostitute.

4

ROUGH
TRADE

This wasn't a glamorous time of my life, but I'm not going to pretend it was horrible either. I spent four months in the house and, although few friendships formed between the boys, there was at least an unspoken empathy. Naturally, there are preconceptions about the sort of people who work in these places and most are spectacularly inaccurate. Generally, male or female sex workers have to be clean and healthy, otherwise it would reflect badly on the business and clients would be discouraged.

Neither were all those I worked alongside gay. I remember one Welsh boy who joined shortly after me, who had recently moved down to London with his girlfriend. She then promptly dumped him, leaving him with nowhere else to go. This saddened me terribly, as although he harboured no resentment towards his choice of work – and I can't say the same was true towards his ex – having sex with men can't have been the most desirable temporary career path for him. Then again, it wasn't top of my list either, and we have to make do with what we can.

Apart from the occasional time I was allowed to sleep in the house, the problem of where to spend each night persisted. Fortunately, I grew close to another boy, Nick, and stayed with him from time to time. A client might on occasion pay for an entire night but, frankly, I never welcomed this, despite the improved income. Physical intimacy was one thing but emotional intimacy quite another, and when an arrangement extended beyond an hour or so that was usually what the customer was after. One night, a gentleman took me back to one of the top suites at the Savoy. I'd never seen such opulence and I was stunned. We'd all heard the stories of how clients had fallen in love with boys and taken them away for a life of unbridled luxury, but as enticing a proposition as it might have sounded, I knew it was never feasible. Even at the Savoy, I could convince neither him nor myself that I was there for anything other than cold, hard cash, and I kept pretending to be asleep. From then on, I decided future appointments would be for an hour or two – but no more.

The overriding problem – which I quickly realised was fully intended by the house – was that we never earned enough to leave the employment. Any income gained just about covered food, expenses and a bed elsewhere for the night. Clients were dissuaded from taking a boy too many times in a day, as this might defeat the purpose and permit him some freedom.

I definitely don't regret my time in South Kensington. I suffered no internal conflicts of guilt or shame, but I didn't want to be tied to an obviously self-destructive cycle. The manager intended to keep me there, with no savings for myself, until he wanted to refresh the stock of workers. After that, I'd just be turfed out into no better a situation than before.

After a string of low-paying days that didn't even cover my essentials, I just upped and left. Not returning the next day meant I wouldn't be allowed in ever again, but I didn't mind in the slightest. I decided to try my luck begging in Covent Garden, to raise a bit more cash so that I could leave England. I needed a new start, and the best way to achieve this seemed to be to get out of the country that caused me so much personal pain, and to rebuild my life from scratch.

Early that evening, I walked to a gay bar called Brief Encounter on St Martin's Lane, and sat against the wall to the side of the main entrance. I'd been in the place a few times and it was reasonably friendly, so I hoped it might be possible to make enough to get a train and ferry to Amsterdam or Berlin. After an hour and the collecting of a few pounds, a lad of my age walked up and smiled. I vaguely recognised him but couldn't remember from where. He introduced himself as Craig, and it turned out he often begged in the place I was sitting. I'd given him a little cash once or twice. Knowing how territorial beggars can be, I mumbled an apology and got up to move on. He gestured for me to stay seated, popped down beside me and asked how I'd found myself there. We chatted and began to beg together, reasoning that the clientele would think we were a couple and give more generously. At the end of the night, incredibly, we'd made nearly £200, which we split before he invited me to his place.

I expected to return to a dingy little flat somewhere in the distant suburbs, but we walked for less than five minutes to an imposing town house in Soho. He led me in and revealed his apartment was the entire top floor! We slept in the same bed and I appreciated his kindness, as he owed me absolutely nothing.

Although Craig was straight, he always chose gay bars. He was a professional beggar and had identified their customers as the nicest and most generous. I asked him how much he made in a week and felt sick when he estimated around £1300. I was struggling merely to stay alive, and he had deliberately chosen begging as his very successful job. He was good-looking, had done his research and hit upon something that required only minimal effort for a few hours each day while sitting down. The inequity of it struck me though, and, having seen the argument from both sides, I do so understand some people's scepticism about beggars.

I don't condemn Craig for what he was doing; he'd identified and exploited an opportunity. He was generous to me, but it wasn't costing him anything, and perhaps he saw me as no threat. As his income was undeclared he wouldn't pay taxes, but a teenager earning in the mid-five figures a year is doing exceptionally well even today. This was all in the late 1980s, so I hope he's had a good life. Meeting Craig did affect me profoundly in one way, though; selling my body was one thing, but sticking my hand out and asking for money was another. Knowing that some people were making a fortune doing just that was too much for my conscience to bear, and I never begged again.

* * *

The seasons changed but my state of affairs didn't – except that, in the summer, my determination to leave the country grew. Having no income and only £100 or so to my name, if I was going to do this it had to be immediately or not at all. I feared it would be the latter, as I still lacked a passport. But I hatched a plan and the next afternoon walked to Liverpool Street station to buy a train ticket to Harwich. A dreary journey passed in under two hours, and I was thankful for the empty carriage. I spent a few hours walking around the Essex town (and yes, I did have to look up which county it's in) until darkness fell. Then I made my way back to the train station and onto the docks.

Years later, the flow of illegal immigrants from the continent would cause security to be significantly tightened around these access points. Yet here I was, trying to escape via the opposite route. The ferries left the port for the Hook of Holland and the first sailing was in eight hours.

I had no trouble getting close to the boat already moored, but was unsure what to do next. Should I try to board now and hide out somewhere, or wait until the crew had disembarked? I reasoned that, while people were allowed access, there was a greater chance of doors being unlocked and finding a place to hunker down unseen. My few possessions were safe in my coat pockets, so I set about my stealthy adventure. Perhaps a little overly dramatic, I crept around corners, hid behind boxes and moved slowly but surely towards the boarding ramp. It was a long, tense hour with my adrenalin and blood pumping hard, but it was also a complete waste of time. I saw not one other person or a single camera.

I expected the early morning sailing to be quiet, but still wanted somewhere inconspicuous to hide. I came across cupboards holding cleaning equipment; they'd conceal me perfectly well, but I didn't want to take the risk. I found the cabins unlocked, but it was just my luck to choose one of the few that was reserved. I looked longingly at the welcoming bed and reluctantly moved on.

Eventually, a couple of floors down, I found a small windowless room featuring nothing more than three chairs and a desk. It didn't seem to be in use and, lying under the desk, I'd be invisible if the door was casually opened. The floor was carpeted and quite warm, so I guessed it was near the engine. I fell asleep and was only woken by the movement of the boat as it left Harwich at dawn.

I was elated at being on my way, nervous about my arrival in Holland, and concerned about being detected. These feelings paled into insignificance against a problem I hadn't considered the night before: I desperately needed to go to the toilet but had no idea of its location, and wanted to avoid being seen. In any chance meeting, I could hardly claim to be a passenger as I was pretty certain they weren't allowed on this deck. That aside, my untidy appearance and nervous disposition would raise suspicions. After all, I was stowing away and trying to enter a sovereign country illegally.

I tried not to think about all the laws I was breaking and to concentrate on my physical discomfort instead. That was a mistake I instantly regretted, as the focus made it intolerable and I couldn't allow any further delay.

I listened at the door and, hearing nothing, my hand hovered by the handle. What if someone passed by at that precise moment? No air of assurance was going to work, so I carefully inched the door open. The corridor was empty so I began my increasingly urgent search. It took a few minutes, but I finally found the gents; to my horror, one of the two cubicles was occupied. I went into the other, locked it and waited. After several literally agonising minutes, I heard a flush and the other man left. Never in my life have I been so relieved, in every possible sense.

I briefly washed, thankful that I'd bought a toothbrush and paste in Harwich. I brushed my teeth with vigour and leaned down to drink water from the tap. Although I was thirsty, I didn't want to take too much as repeating this hazardous bathroom trip might be a step too far. My bladder would just have to wait until we reached dry land.

I hurried back to the room without getting lost, hearing disembodied voices as I did so. I hadn't seen a clock, but guessed I had five further hours or so stuck under my desk. I didn't know how long the ship would be docked, but if it were heading back to England that afternoon, I wouldn't have long to get off.

Sitting patiently for extended periods is not something I've ever been good at. I don't do beach holidays, even with a big pile of books, as I've always got to be doing something. I've been asked what I'll do when I retire and the very thought appals me. That would be equivalent to death and that, my dear fellow, shall be the very last thing I do!

After a while I wanted to get up and explore, so I began

imagining what might happen if I was caught. Human curiosity is insatiable, but I managed to hold mine in check. I'd have plenty of opportunities when I reached Amsterdam, so I grudgingly kept my head down and waited.

I won't pretend I was racked with anxiety at finding myself in this little cabin, because I wasn't. I was still only eighteen and this was a *Boy's Own* adventure, albeit a most uncertain one.

In due course the boat pulled up at the Hook. Now I had to make another decision. The lay of the land outside was a mystery to me, but time was clearly of the essence. I couldn't get off with the passengers as I'd inevitably be noticed, and passport officials could meet us at any moment. I waited half an hour or so and ventured out of my hiding place, suddenly realising I'd have to hunt for the exit. The ship may have travelled with minimum staff, but they were likely all aboard preparing for the return trip, and I needed to remain unseen.

I climbed the first two staircases I saw, hoping I was now on the correct level. Several times I heard talking but was lucky enough to avoid anyone in person. I found the way out but heard a group of people speaking close by. There was another toilet opposite so I went in, leaving the door ajar until I was sure the coast was clear.

The voices soon faded as two men strode onto land, retreating into the distance. I looked around the corner and saw the immigration building unnervingly close, only twenty metres or so from the ship. I could see officers inside, relaxing after dealing with the full registered complement of customers. I scurried down the ramp, around a corner, behind a row of lorries and found myself in the Netherlands.

My first port of call had to be the train station. This was clearly marked and close to the terminal. I hadn't the faintest grasp of Dutch but was reasonably hopeful that everyone would be able to converse in English. I was shocked, therefore, when I tried to buy a train ticket to the capital city. It wasn't that the staff didn't speak English; it was that they spoke it so fluently. I came to learn that, although it is taught in schools from age twelve, it's perhaps the most pointless lesson ever. English is all-pervasive throughout the world – especially in Holland, where the BBC is received and programmes are subtitled rather than dubbed. All children are completely fluent by their teenage years, and I met several who spoke it better than many English adults.

I bought my ticket – grateful that sterling was accepted but worried that I only had £30 left – settled into my wonderfully bouncy train seat and enjoyed the brief journey. I was bound for Amsterdam, a city that had intrigued me for years with its reputation for being so welcoming, tolerant and culturally exciting. As I pulled into Central Station, I thought this might be the very place I'd be happy to call home. Those thoughts proved prophetic, as a staircase in the station would end up being my home for the next fifteen months.

It was a wet, early Saturday evening when I stepped out into Amsterdam city centre. The main road, the Damrak, stretched ahead of me and I stood staring in wonder at the canals and buildings. I began thinking about spending my first weekend alone in a foreign country. The initial anticipation had died; I was dispirited by the rain but at least it was still light, so I walked for a few minutes before returning to the station. I was going to have to exchange my remaining cash in order to buy anything, so I found a kiosk, tried not to resent the low tourist rate on offer and departed with a handful of guilders.

It's worth mentioning here how beautiful the paper currency of the Netherlands used to be. The notes were exquisite works of art, and I particularly recall the hundred guilders, which were brown and had a stunning picture of a snipe. I'm all for European integration, but I bemoan some of the individual beauty that's been lost. That was all for the future, however. My current fund was insufficient for even one of the 100-guilder notes I came to admire so much.

I bought a cone of chips topped with a huge, creamy dollop of mayonnaise and wolfed them down as I strolled wide-eyed down the Damrak. My mission was to learn where local bars were located, so I asked at an information stand and was directed to an area where a few were clustered together. Not looking my best, I chose one, strode in, ordered a bottle of water and sat in the bar area, confident my youth would at least garner plenty of attention. I smiled, made eye contact, looked interested and enjoyed the music. I sent out all the right signals and wondered how to make my choice from the long list of offers I anticipated.

By midnight, nobody had spoken to me, and it was increasingly difficult to slip to the bathroom and top up my water bottle without anyone noticing. Flicking through a magazine, I saw ads for an all-night sauna; it sounded very appealing but would require a big chunk of what little money I had. There again, it was open and would stay so until morning, when free coffee was served. A warm, comfortable night where I might even meet someone long-term seemed like a good bet, so I made my way the few blocks down to Kerkstraat. This was all very thrilling, even slightly naughty, and I began to feel free of my British inhibitions.

The man on the door questioned me about my age, but relaxed when it was clear I was English and therefore presumably a tourist. It was a very clean, professional-looking place situated over several floors, and I was delighted that the bathrooms supplied razors and other toiletries. I used what I wanted and stuffed my coat pockets full of extras. I had a ridiculously long, hot shower and finally felt ready to face other people. For the first time in ages I looked respectable; after the sauna, steam room and whirlpool had relaxed me, I ventured excitedly upstairs to the private cabins.

The place was already pretty busy so my expectations were high. I laid back in one of the rooms, pushing the door half-closed to tempt visitors and promptly fell asleep. The next thing I remember was a loudspeaker blaring that coffee was being served in the bar and the building would be closing in half an hour. Although I was clean and rested, I viewed the whole evening as a wasted opportunity I'd be unable to afford again. I consumed my bodyweight in free coffee and biscuits before getting dressed and leaving. It was a Sunday morning in Amsterdam and still raining.

I had a plan in mind but could do nothing until the next day. I wandered around for a few hours, vaguely looking for shops or free galleries where I could stay dry. Back then, however, most businesses closed from Saturday afternoon to Monday lunchtime, so virtually nothing was open. The few museums I found charged entry fees and I wasn't about to squander my precious few notes.

At least I had a gorgeous city to look at. I was drawn by the incredible and imaginative architecture around every corner. Each building had its own little surprises; even now, when I return, I find myself looking upward and marvelling. We invariably miss so much as we shuffle around, eyes firmly fixed on the pavement or our smartphones. This is one little piece of advice I like to impart to anyone willing to listen: when you're walking along, crane your neck backwards for a moment. Incredible details are free to view every day, just above our heads. Please look up and I promise you won't regret it.

As the day progressed, I had to preserve as much money as possible, so I satisfied myself with a packet of crusty bread rolls from the supermarket, costing a few cents. I'd kept myself hydrated by drinking from the taps in public toilets, but as evening closed in, it was time to buy another bottle of water at the bar and try my luck once more. At least this time I was clean-shaven and looked fresher, so I sat at the same bar, hoping someone might recognise me from the night before and strike up a conversation.

I'm not about to blame anyone but myself for my difficulty in handling social situations. Even now, I prefer the anonymous faces in a crowd of thousands to a small group of strangers. I'm fine once I get on personal terms, but the terror of that initial stage is so insurmountable that I rarely get beyond it. I've never had many friends and, even now, have virtually no self-confidence, so you can imagine how I felt back then!

I'd never dream of starting a conversation with people I don't know, because I always assume that if they had any interest in talking to me, they'd do so. My default setting is that no one will want to spend time with me. This works most of the time, but can lead to huge problems if the other party is persistent. When I fell in love later in life and that love was returned, I was a spectacular moron, hurtful and aggressive, trying to scare him away. I'm eternally grateful that he was able to see through my actions and stayed by me. In his position, I can't believe anyone else would have been so loving and resilient. I certainly wouldn't have been, but that's why he's a better man than I could ever be. However, we'll get to that man in a mere nine years' time...

Back then, I saw other guys chatting to each other, but there was no way I was going to be able to start any conversation. Over the course of the evening, as the bar became busier, I grew more sullen. People around me got happier, but I began scowling; realising I was defeating my own ambitions, I soon departed. I had nowhere to go and couldn't afford another visit to the sauna. I slouched back to Central Station, which was still busy with the night crowd, and found a quiet staircase off the left of the main hall. I pulled my coat around me, leaned against the wall and closed my eyes. I had somewhere important to be in eight hours and wanted as much rest as possible before I got there.

The sun rose early and slowly illuminated my hiding place from a skylight above my head. I blinked in the sun's rays with sadness, as I hadn't managed a single second of sleep. I felt utterly drained and annoyed. I walked into the station, which was as busy as the last time I'd seen it, but this time with commuters. As I passed onto the concourse, a beggar asked me for some change and I distractedly shook my head.

He responded very aggressively and swore at me, a reaction I never forgot. It was my first experience of a homeless person in another country and it was anything but positive.

I headed across the city centre to find the British Embassy. The right course of action was to be honest about what I'd done, despite the risk of being sent back and punished. Therefore, I decided not to lie but employ a degree of embellishment to elicit sympathy. It was obvious that I was in the country without permission, and any story about having my passport stolen could easily be checked. I therefore spun a story about constant physical threats from gangs in London, and having to escape overnight.

The whole thing was preposterous and the staff knew it. I was young, well spoken and in need of help, but none of these factors seemed to carry much weight. Fortunately, I was in Holland, which is a cosmopolitan country with inclusive legislation, and as soon as I told them I was gay their mood brightened considerably. They may not have actually cared, but I was now a welcome tick on some list, which proved sufficient to push me to the front of the queue. The fact that I was apparently the only visitor in the embassy all day made me wonder if they were just glad to have something to concentrate on.

After a few hours, my identity was confirmed and I was presented with a full, brand-new British passport, printed right there in the building. I then unintentionally trampled all over their work by asking how I could change my name. The lady attending to me patiently explained all the official procedures. Officialdom hadn't yet extinguished her kindness, and she whispered that there were always ways around it. She understood my motivation and gave me some inside tips that would prove invaluable later on.

I'd now taken the first tentative step to rebuilding my life. I spent all day at the embassy and the staff, much to my surprise, couldn't have been more helpful. I got plenty of useful information, including the address of Leger des Heils, the Dutch branch of the Salvation Army. I decided to try it for a bed and found the building in the heart of the infamous Red Light District. I was lucky that the first volunteer I met there was English, about thirty, gay and fully appreciative of my problems.

(As a little sidebar, why is it that so many men in the caring fields are gay? I've never believed that one's sexuality has any bearing on one's character. Neither intelligence nor creativity has anything to do with it either, so why should this be the case? The entertainment and – perhaps surprisingly – information technology industries also seem to have disproportionately large gay contingents, and I've never been able to fathom it out. It's not important, but it fascinates me!)

I was offered a bed at Leger des Heils that evening, but it was, predictably, in a large room sharing with over twenty other men. Most were in a pretty bad way as the house policy was to turn no one away, irrespective of personal or addiction problems. I was scared but the prospect of a real bed was a rare luxury, and I didn't want to turn it down. There was a communal dining hall, but food was served later in the evening. As the only choices were to walk the streets aimlessly or sit there in the warmth, the latter won.

I noticed two men playing chess so I asked if I could watch. They agreed and joked that I could help if I thought I could play. Almost immediately, one man made an illegal move and I pointed this out. His temper flipped as quickly as the board and he started screaming at me. It wasn't in any language I recognised, but I doubt he was politely thanking me for my contribution to the game.

Some moments just stay with you forever and this was one I would never forget. He was a frightening character, almost a caricature of a typical tramp, and this affected me more than the shouting. I saw a possible glimmer of my own future in his tired eyes and I was suddenly very sad. Despite a certainty that I deserved something better, perhaps in reality this was all I could look forward to. I tried to avoid the inevitable question, but eventually confronted it and frankly asked myself if there was really any point in going on.

I spoke to the volunteer at the Salvation Army and thanked him for his help, but explained that I couldn't really stay there. I'd be too scared, as what little money I had, along with my precious passport, was stuffed into my underpants for safekeeping.

I actually hoped he was going to offer to let me stay at his place, but he didn't and who could blame him? I was an anonymous face off the street to him, and the security of his home and person had to come first. We chatted for a while and arranged to meet for a drink the next evening. Bright instances like that can give so much hope; I had something to look forward to and, although it was over twenty hours away, it was a small beacon of light to aim towards.

I trudged back in the general direction of the station and was hugely disappointed when I reached it in less than ten minutes. I hadn't realised I was so close, and the whole area was still heavy with people. The interminable waiting for the rare mercy of sleep is an awful burden when you're homeless. This, combined with the daily uncertainty, weighs heavily, and it's no surprise that so many find themselves unable, or unwilling, to cope.

I turned away and passed down a road that ran alongside the Damrak. I passed the Crowne Plaza hotel on my left, and wondered what sort of fabulous people must have been within its walls. I wasn't jealous, as I'd solemnly accepted my life for all it was, and at least had the consolation that things may get better. And indeed they would, but only after getting a hell of a lot worse...

I passed a townhouse on my right that attracted my attention. Virtually all the old seventeenth-century houses lean one way or another in central Amsterdam; this one, however, lurched forwards more alarmingly, though seemingly as securely as the rest. From a return trip twenty-five years later I can report it's still there, tottering at the same precarious angle that I remember. The entire building was painted black, which was unusual but by no means unique. What stood out was a bright neon sign just above the door, declaring the building to be 'Blue Boy'. I imagined it was a nightclub, but as nothing else was visible I got no further than that.

I kept on my way, fascinated by the trams that rattled along the centre of the roads. As I got to know the systems in Holland and Germany, I learned to appreciate the chaotic beauty of how trams, traffic and pedestrians worked together. Trams take the centre alongside taxis, with other traffic on either side. There are far more pedestrian crossings than in Britain and, even if traffic is moving through a green light, pedestrians have right of way. The cars patiently wait their turn.

Though intimidating at first, I quickly adjusted to the elegance of the traffic system. City accidents are very rare and the roads remain safe for most users. Of course, in Amsterdam the stereotypical bicycle is a phenomenon. As in Britain, they're not allowed on pavements but cycle lanes are common, and there are relatively few cars anyway. The main problems are the almost total lack of helmets and the passengers who balance precariously and unsecured on the basket shelf to the rear of the bikes. They weave in and out of car and foot traffic and, unsurprisingly, injuries are more common. During my first stay in Amsterdam, the cyclists' antics terrified me, but now I'm just terrified by their indifference to basic safety.

I found myself in Dam Square when a young man whistled at me, interrupting my absent-minded looking around. I turned and he nodded smilingly with a gesture towards the statue that dominates the square. I followed him tentatively and was suddenly surrounded by him and three colleagues. They pulled out little sachets of drugs and put their hands out, demanding money. I turned to get away but one grabbed my arm. I started pleading to make it clear I was a confused tourist, but where gentle persuasion failed they were convinced that overt threats would work.

I was already genuinely scared when one pulled out a small knife. I was so glad that my money was concealed and resorted to the only option that came to mind, screaming at the top of my voice. Several people turned to look, and this was clearly not the attention that the four men craved.

Stuffing their hands away, they quickly strode off. I learned later that the Dam is where many drug deals are arranged. Young men, often from North Africa, congregate there to sell to tourists and locals. Incredibly, it still goes on, as it was tried on me several times on my most recent trip.

(If you do go to Amsterdam, please, for your own safety, completely ignore anyone who tries to get your attention in this way.)

Shortly after, still shaken, I arrived back at my station staircase and settled down. My passport was tucked away in a very sensitive position, but I was now fearful of every noise and shadow. There was no way I would dare to remove such a vital item, so I endured the discomfort. After the lack of respite the previous night, I was hopeful that, the relatively early hour aside, I would be able to sleep this time. Although they were very fitful and disturbed, I did in fact manage a few very welcome hours of rest.

The next morning was cold but amazingly rain free. It was too early even for the bakeries to open, so I took advantage of the quietness to visit the station bathrooms. There was an entry charge but, with no staff on duty, I skipped over the barriers to save a little of my ever-dwindling coinage. I washed and made myself as ready for the day as feasible, focused on meeting my Salvation Army friend later.

The day was uneventful and intolerably boring, as I was now getting accustomed to. There was a complete lack of activities with which to occupy myself. I also had to bear in mind factors most people wouldn't even think about. I didn't want to walk around constantly, as I was mindful about wearing out my shoes; with no chance of acquiring another pair I had to take great care. Two guilders to spend an hour in a warm museum may not have felt like much, but even that meagre amount would have accounted for a large chunk of what I had left. I tried to avoid the busy areas, as I must have looked pretty strange strolling around with a packet of crusty rolls stuffed under my arm. There was also the worry, however unlikely, of bumping into someone I knew. I was keen for this to be avoided at all costs.

Finally, it was time to meet, and even though I was aching all over I was excited to see a friendly face. We met at the Downtown coffee shop and he bought me a huge, steamy Americano. As I warmed my hands around it, he asked me how I'd ended up in Amsterdam.

I hesitated to tell him at first. After all, why should he believe me? However, his work had made him used to tales of woe far worse than mine. I spilled out my story and was thankful that he neither demurred nor appeared shocked at any point.

I don't know what I was expecting from him, but at the back of my mind I was hoping he'd take me back to his flat. I didn't find him physically attractive, but then I wasn't up to much myself at the time, and he probably viewed me in the same way. Nevertheless, he was nice, friendly and had a warm bed. I wasn't in a position to be choosy but the eventuality never arose anyway.

He asked me how much money I had and I truthfully answered about seventy guilders (around £25). Even with my current living arrangements this wouldn't last long, and malnutrition was a concern at the back of my mind. I had no right to expect to be cared for by the Dutch government, as they would quite rightly insist I return to Britain. I now had a passport so I was qualified only for very limited help. As I was hardly a refugee, I had to stop moaning and go back home.

Except that was the whole point: I didn't have a home and had never had one. I'd always been alone and was well aware that was to be my fate. Frankly, if I'd been presented with the cold, hard options of returning or fending for myself, I would have stayed firmly put.

He asked me if I'd heard of the Blue Boy. I said I'd passed the place earlier by chance and presumed it was a club, but he shook his head and told me it was a gay brothel. He also said it was pretty much my only option. I nodded and, even with no guarantee that they'd take me, thanked him for his kind advice. He was only trying to be supportive. and it was clearly all I was going to get from him.

I can't express how much I didn't want to go down that path again. I'd hoped that part of my life was over as, unlike Craig's begging in Covent Garden, it was hardly a lucrative, long-term career for me.

I casually tried once more to wangle an invitation to his flat. I explained how all I needed was a couple of days to get my mind together and sort out what I needed. In my twisted imagination, I saw him grudgingly giving in and letting me stay awhile. He'd then fall so madly in love with me that he couldn't bear to let me leave, and we'd live together happily. It sounds insultingly opportunistic now but, having lived desperately and precariously for a year and a half, I was willing to grasp at whatever flimsy straws I could.

It was getting late so he made his excuses and left. I

mustered the bravest face I was able to, but felt angry and confused. Why hadn't he helped me? What the hell was I supposed to do now?

Of course, he had helped me and was under no obligation to do anything further – especially as he didn't really know me. There was an informal invitation to drop in and see him at work whenever I wanted. I did this a few times; our chats were friendly but all too brief. Soon I began calling round almost every day, if only because I had nowhere else to go and nothing else to do. The other staff might say he wasn't there, but then I'd just hang around the doorway, vaguely waiting. I suspect he was already in the building but, like a very bad penny, I was turning up far too often. If that was the case, I apologise for outstaying my welcome – but then I don't believe loving natures like his really hold grudges.

A couple of weeks passed and my days were reduced to nothing more than repetitive exercises in avoiding death. Life is undeniably important, but so is quality of life, and I began to fret that to me this was an unattainable dream. My money was almost gone and I had nothing to look forward to or to work towards. With no light on the horizon to hold out for, there seemed to be absolutely no point. If I didn't make a drastic change, I was going to die as a teenager and no one would care, or even notice.

This thought upset me, but it was soon subsumed by anger. My death was exactly what all those people from my youth had repeatedly said they wanted! I wasn't about to give any of those bastards the satisfaction...

I had my friend's home number, so I wanted to call to tell him I'd decided to try the Blue Boy. I'd put it off as long as possible but, with no viable alternative, decided to make the best of it. I found a phone box by a quiet canal near the university and dialled.

As the phone rang, there was a tapping on the glass behind me. A withered man, maybe in his fifties but he could have been much older, was standing there. He was dishevelled, emaciated, with a scruffy, unwashed beard. I opened the door and, as he stood pathetically there, he glanced nervously to each side before pulling out a knife. He weakly demanded I give him all my money and anything of value.

I should have laughed, as one hand would have been more than sufficient to overpower him. He may have been a long-gone drug addict trying to get his latest fix, but unfortunately he picked the wrong person at the wrong time.

I completely snapped, dropped the phone and flew at him in fury. He didn't expect this reaction and was immediately thrown into terror. I grabbed the knife, tossed it into the water and started to thump him. I screamed the entire time, allowing all my frustration and hurt to flood out. I couldn't help myself, but doubt that I even wanted to. He'd tried, however meekly, to mug me at knifepoint and I was just defending myself.

Of course this is ludicrous, as the gentlest of slaps would have got rid of him. Once unarmed, he'd hardly be a threat to anyone else. But my assault continued until I half-punched, half-pushed him into the canal. Trembling with rage and with fists still tightly clenched, I'm ashamed to say I walked away. I didn't give this sorry creature another thought.

I was unsure whether to write about this incident. On balance, I've decided to do so as it reveals a very unpleasant side of my character, and I'm determined to be totally honest. Portraying myself as a perpetual victim would be unworthy, defeating the whole purpose of putting words on paper. I abhor all forms of violence and offer no defence, except that decades of abuse and pain had bottled up so much rage that it resulted in one terrible outburst.

I'm disgusted by what I was reduced to in that brief moment. I can rationalise every other choice made in those days, but my response to this half-hearted crime was disproportionate and unforgiveable. I've said before that there was nothing in my life I regretted. In writing this difficult passage, I'm coming to terms with the fact that I was lying...

I was in no mood to be around respectable people and felt more of an outcast than ever before. I hurried through the backstreets, doing my best to avoid anybody I saw before arriving at the station. The back of the building overlooks the water, so it was relatively quiet. I huddled down in a doorway, still in a state of shock, and didn't move for hours.

Eventually, the cold forced me back inside to my usual place, where I steadfastly remained throughout the night. I think two further days passed before my head was shaken back to any sense of normality, as ignoring my worsening situation wasn't doing much good. I was down to mere pennies, with my list of options reduced to one. I sneaked back into the bathrooms and did what I could to freshen myself up. Shaving in tepid water without foam or a towel isn't recommended, but I had to do something to make myself appear young and presentable.

(Being clean-shaven is important, as I discovered many years later. In a play, I was cast as a character much older than me, and growing a beard significantly aged me. It was also perhaps the most unpleasant thing I've ever done. It itched unmercifully, and brushing my teeth resulted in a big, foamy mass covering my entire lower face. After a meal I'd be picking food out of the hair for hours, but worst of all was when the bristles on my upper lip grew so long that they reached down into my mouth! No disrespect to any of my hirsute friends, but a beard is most definitely not for me.)

I bought some bread and cheese from the supermarket for much-needed sustenance as I walked around. I was in no way happy, but at least making a choice, however distasteful, had given me a sense of direction. My actions of two days ago weighed heavily, but I'd had enough of permanent suffering. If I wanted to survive, I had to stand up and take control. I've always striven to be kind, but right then I had to compete in the human race.

I was still only eighteen, so hopefully I'd be young and appealing enough for the Blue Boy to take me, although there was also the nagging reservation that I'd be turned away. Perhaps they didn't want any English boys, or were already full. Either way, I wanted to at least try and change my glass half-empty mentality, trying not to dwell on the prospect of failure.

I waited until early afternoon, walked to the black house and rang the bell. A man answered in Dutch, but I apologised for not understanding and asked if they had any vacancies. The door clicked open and I went up a narrow flight of stairs to be met by an ominous-looking, bald, overweight man in his fifties. He pleasantly introduced himself as the manager, and explained I'd have to complete an application. This basically meant having sex with him.

It lasted a few hours, and for the whole time I kept in mind the money I anticipated earning after this ordeal. I also feared being turned down after all this, as I'd be powerless to do anything about it if I was. But by early evening it was over and I was permitted to stay.

I was shown into the bar area and sat with a few other boys from all over Europe, as we waited for clients to arrive. The Blue Boy stayed open until early morning, and even a little cash each day would cover a stay at the night sauna afterwards. It wasn't much of an existence but at least it was a definite plan.

The major flaw lay in expecting to make money, which was never going to be easy. The competition between the boys was ruthless and the manager would always steer clients towards his favourites, which didn't include me. I was one of the very youngest boys there but several – especially those from Czechoslovakia for some reason – looked a lot more youthful, even when in their early twenties.

I was lucky if I managed £15 a day, which sufficed for the sauna and a small amount of food. I worked it out on a daily basis, depending on my hunger and how cold the weather was. If I wanted a big, warming meal, it was back to the station. If I wanted a warm sleep, and maybe sex, I headed for Kerkstraat. As winter was drawing in, these decisions gained more urgency. Amsterdam is a fairly cold, wet city at the best of times, but, because of its natural geography, the coastline around it acts as a natural wind tunnel. The air temperature is always misleading. The wind chill can be biting, and my sleeping spot on the stone staircase of a large building, open to the elements, was never much of a refuge.

What else was I to do? My agitation was edged with sadness but I was never self-pitying; if this was my life, so be it. I would prefer to die where I was than to return to a country where all I'd ever known was hatred and violence. At least I could take control, and my last days would be lived under my own terms.

Even when I chose the sauna, it was usually only to shower and go straight to sleep. If I arrived at one in the morning, I only had six hours until the alarm went off to signal coffee and imminent closing, so it was hardly a relaxed environment. But I always shaved and took advantage of the free supplies before heading out into the morning cold.

My nineteenth birthday passed unnoticed, and I continued to scrape together what I could. The Blue Boy opened at noon so I'd be there on the dot to try and catch any rare lunchtime clients, an exertion many of the other boys weren't interested in. It rarely worked for me either, but I was elated when it did and at least it was warm inside.

December arrived and so did an enormous problem. The manager suddenly announced he was disappearing on holiday in ten days' time, until the New Year. We assumed he would leave someone else in charge, but he reasoned that it wasn't worth the effort over the quiet holiday period and decided to shut shop for a few weeks.

This was horrible news and it came without warning. With a heads up, I'd have saved a few more guilders, but, as with the London brothel, the boys were constantly on edge. I spent every second of the next week and a half trying to make whatever I could, but even then there were very slim pickings.

Everyone else felt the urgency, and I was no longer alone

for the first couple of hours of business. A group of us congregated impatiently outside the door as it opened each midday, but by the time the manager left, I had only enough to support myself for three or four days. I couldn't see any hope now, and seriously doubted that I'd last out the year.

One boy I worked alongside was from Spain. I can't remember his name but he was a year or so older than me, with bleached-blond hair. We were walking in the Vondelpark to the south of the city centre, with nowhere to go. There were holiday decorations everywhere, and lots of happy faces flitted by in flashes of light and laughter. We were denied any share of this, and it was keenly felt by us both.

All at once he turned to me and declared he didn't want to go on anymore. I suggested sitting down, but knew that wasn't what he meant. We were on friendly terms and had spent time together, but we weren't particularly close, so what he said next shocked me: he asked if I would go with him.

It took a few moments for me to grasp his meaning. My first instinct was to ask how on earth he could contemplate such a thing – for him or me. But my words remained unspoken and he continued to look at me sadly. If I knew this was all there was, and neither of us apparently deserved any better, then why was I bothering to fight? I wanted to argue against his reasoning but stayed speechless. Once again, the phrase 'on my own terms' echoed through my head.

We delved deeper into the park, which is immense. There are lakes, houses, large open spaces, hidden grottoes and playgrounds within its huge boundary. After the longest while of not speaking we found a quiet spot, a solitary bench by a small, wooden bridge over a pond, all enclosed and hidden by tall trees.

We sat down together and held hands, neither being able, or willing, to say anything. We were both scared but he was less so, as his mind was made up. I daren't imagine what he had planned, but then he pulled a small bag from inside his coat and I looked down to see five very strange pills. They were pale pink in colour, and they were enormous. Each must have been nearly an inch long and quite thick. Even thinking of swallowing them almost made me gag.

I asked what they were but he seemed reluctant to tell me – or perhaps he simply didn't know. The only word he was sure about was 'horse' which, however obtuse considering the situation, I found absurdly comical. Was he seriously offering me a horse tranquiliser or something similar? Where on earth had he got these from and, although the result of taking them might be pretty conclusive, what effect would they have until then?

However, in the shared harshness of the weather and mood at the time, it all seemed brutally clear and logical. He had a cheap and simple way to end his life and he wanted me, with my equally bleak prospects, to go with him. He didn't want to be alone and was presenting an easy solution. We'd take the tablets, sit on the bench, hands clasped together, and just wait.

He took one out, passed it to me and I took it in my hand without comment. I held it tightly in my fist and grabbed his left hand, forcing him to struggle to retrieve a second tablet for himself. We sat frozen, and I stared intently at the pond, waiting for the fateful instruction.

Life, for all its routines and certainties, is rarely obvious, and never less so than when it comes to its end. We had nothing to live for, but still I was reluctant to check out. Surely there must have been something more to it. Even if I wasn't worth another chance, didn't I owe it to myself to find out? The passage from *Schindler's Ark* came back to me, as it had done so often in the past. And I can nobly excuse it as much as I like, but the basic fact is that I was petrified.

Not about death itself, as it holds absolutely no mystery for me. You die, you rot, and that's it: no soul and definitely no afterlife. There's no nothingness to eternally float around in, because there's nothing of you left to experience the nothingness. Life flickers in you just once and leaves you just once, after an all-too-brief interlude. That is all there is.

My fear sprang from how I was going to die. If a quick, painless death awaited me, and my last feeling would be the touch of someone who at least wanted to share that defining moment with me, then it was no problem. It sounds terrible to say it, but I very nearly committed suicide that day, and it was only the threat of prolonged pain that stopped me.

All the people who'd never meet or love me would hardly be poorer for an unknown absence; their lives would continue quite oblivious to the snuffing out of one insignificant light. At the time though, my sole worry was if it was going to hurt. I asked the boy and he shrugged his shoulders, neither knowing nor caring. He'd chosen his dark path and how to go down it. A tablet so big that it must be fatal, I supposed, but after how long?

I really didn't want to be writhing around in agony for ages until my organs finally gave up. I tried to argue this point, as it was hardly the peaceful image we'd conjured up. I detested the idea of him taking the ultimate step alone, but not enough to enter the chasm at his side. So many young men feel compelled to take their own lives; each one is a tragedy, and I very nearly became another forgotten statistic.

But I pulled back, and I yearned to do the same for him. He was the closest thing I had to a friend, and I implored him so that we could stay together and support each other. As friends, lovers or boyfriends, we could start anew and build a life together, but my entreaties were useless.

We were both in tears at this breaking point. He shouted at me in choked Spanish, so the words were lost on me. The hurt in his voice and his eyes, however, was unmistakeable. He ran off, ignoring my pleas – which of course were more selfish than altruistic

He was the sole positive aspect in my life, and I was desperate to hold onto him but knew I'd lost my chance. In his eyes I'd betrayed him and destroyed what he saw as his only chance to share something meaningful with another person.

I stayed seated for the longest time, before standing up and gently dropping the tablet into the water. I looked in the direction he'd gone off in, but I never saw him again. I am truly mortified that I can't recall more about him. Some people deserve so much more than to be a nameless memory.

*   *   *

My clothes were falling to pieces about me and barely saw me through the winter. I never returned to begging, but the blatant trauma I was going through was obvious to the wonderful Dutch commuters who often left coins uninvited. I regularly checked the Blue Boy for signs of life, until one day, towards the end of January, a notice appeared on the door to say it would reopen the next week. This was clearly for the benefit of the boys, as Kai was all too aware of how to manipulate and keep his staff keen.

I was so thrilled, which sounds ridiculous to me now. I was actually getting my hopes up at the prospect of selling my body for a pittance, but those were the crumbs I had to scramble for. I survived until the promised day and was waiting excitedly outside the door from early morning. Other boys joined me, most of whom I'd seen before, until we were allowed in.

The new faces were ushered off to await their interview, but the manager stopped me as I tried to push in. I was unsuitable, he said, no longer up to his standard. I begged him to change his mind. Perhaps he enjoyed this little flex of managerial power, but I could see his point. I was malnourished, dirty, covered in spots and rotting clothes. My teenage years and a very limited diet were unkind to my complexion and body.

I proposed staying a day or two to see how things panned out. He finally relented. But then, either by his design or due to my appearance, I didn't get a sniff of any work and was astute enough to accept this wasn't likely to change. I left dejectedly at the end of the second day, with no acknowledgment from the manager or any other boy.

I spent a further nine months in Amsterdam, always cold, always hungry, always alone. On one hand it became easier, as the weather warmed, but this was outweighed by the increasing bustle of the city. All day long the mass of bodies heaved, bloated by the growing influx of tourists. The station and city centre were busier from much earlier until much later. Refuge was difficult to find but I was grateful that, unlike in Britain, the police never moved me on. I kept hidden and they had better things to attend to.

One older policewoman was greatly conflicted, as she came to see me regularly. She knew I had no issues with drugs or alcohol, and was just a young kid forced onto the streets, but her professionalism prevented her getting too involved. From time to time though, she was unable to resist and her random acts of kindness are something I'll never forget. She never introduced herself but brought me food and drink several times. Buying a couple of extra items on her break if she saw me around was enough, but the occasional treat was also smuggled from home. The most valuable gifts were a long scarf and a pair of boots, presented in exchange for a solemn promise that I'd never reveal the donor. I hope, after all this time, that she'll forgive the indiscretion and accept my heartfelt thanks. The boots were a little too small but they were priceless to me, as the scraps hanging off my feet were only fit for the bin.

I've never known a country as forthright in its personal generosity as the Netherlands. The Dutch are so kind and open, and demand nothing in return. Their loving nature exists simply for its own sake, and I doubt I'd be writing this now if I'd been in any other country. Every year I return to Amsterdam for a few days, to enjoy myself and pay my respects in my own quiet way. Even though I went through torture for weeks and months on end, I've never been anywhere else that feels as much like a home as Amsterdam. I've travelled the globe and seen many wondrous places, but the question of my favourite city is settled.

With this connection in mind, I often contemplated changing my name. I needed to erase all reminders of the people and events of the past. I'd toyed around with initials for my forename and liked 'CJ', so that stuck, but the surname was trickier. I wanted to honour the country and its people by choosing something Dutch, but my knowledge of the language was very patchy, so something that tripped off the tongue was the best option. I always favour the more unusual, and 'de Mooi' just looked and sounded right. As a full name, 'CJ de Mooi' was aesthetically pleasing, so after a few weeks' mulling, my choice was confirmed.

(Surprisingly, this would cause a minor controversy many years later when I gained a public profile. With only my television persona as a reference, many people criticised me for the surname. It translates as 'the pretty' in Dutch, and this was seen as a damning indictment of my arrogance and smugness. Well, if my character is that convincing on screen, thank you – I'll take my BAFTA to go. But the timeline is pretty evident: the name was in place long before I settled in Amsterdam in 1995, which was when I finally became confident in the native tongue. I simply liked the name and that's why I picked it.)

Time crawled by, with the station staircase greeting my backside virtually every night. If I was lucky enough to find enough coins had been dropped at my feet, the night sauna awaited – but that was usually a once-a-month luxury. My hair was overgrown, my beard patchy, my nails hideous and my body odour indescribable. I was emaciated but, on the positive side, my spots had cleared up – so every cloud has a silver lining!

The summer and autumn were pretty warm, which was a welcome relief. But everywhere was packed with tourists, most of who appeared to be English. Before the Baltic countries took over, thanks to the advent of budget airlines, Amsterdam was the destination of choice for British stag parties. These were a nightmare that I had to avoid. Rough sleepers encountering these drunken moveable feasts in London would be wary, but here it was terrifying. Freed from the shackles of a domestic police service, their behaviour recognised no boundaries. I stayed out of sight as best I could, but twice I woke up to find members of these hideous groups urinating on me. This is how they treated fellow human beings; I couldn't imagine Dutchmen doing the same.

I did what I could to clean myself up but my body was rarely the problem. My one set of clothes, in which I had no choice but to live permanently, was stained and stinking. Water and hand soap from the bathroom offered only a mild reprieve; even constant washing failed to eradicate the lingering smell of urine from my hair.

Mid-October arrived and I reflected that I'd been in Amsterdam for over a year, the vast majority of which I'd spent in the very same place. I'd even become quite attached to my specific step, as it was the centre of my world and a fixed point. In difficult situations we cling to whatever constants we can, and this pathetic little space was mine.

In two weeks, I'd cease to be a teenager, and I didn't

relish the prospect of starting my twenties in the same mess. It wasn't a case of the grass being greener elsewhere, but the next few days persuaded me to find some new pastures. Returning to Britain was never an option, so I decided to plunge deeper into the continent. As I spoke some of the language and it was geographically close, Germany was my first choice.

Despite deciding on the very cosmopolitan Cologne, I doubted English would be as prevalent as I'd been used to. A train journey of slightly over two hours was impractical with only a few cents, so I tried to hitchhike. This was a serious mistake for two reasons: I hadn't the remotest clue which road led to Cologne, and hitchhiking is relatively rare in Europe. Of course, it happens in those delightful commercials where fresh-faced blond backpackers enjoy the Alps with their ruddy cheeks and happy smiles. I didn't quite match that description and my attempts were wholly unsuccessful. Now, when I give lifts to anyone I can, even I'd think twice at picking up such a ghoulish figure by the side of the road, so I can hardly blame drivers for not stopping.

Jumping on the train without a ticket remained my sole option. I figured the worst they could do was put me off at the next station and, if it was an intercity, that might actually be where I was going! The default setting of waving my passport and feigning ignorance would be doomed to fail but boarding presented no issues, as what few ticket barriers there were could be easily hopped over and surveillance hardly existed.

I planned one last brief sleep on my trusty step before making my way onto the platform and jumping the first train I could.

The quieter and earlier I made it, the less chance there was of ticket guards. Next morning, I waited as nonchalantly as I could – discreetly leaning against a snack kiosk, out of sight – for the train to arrive from Paris just after 6am. The sleek carriages slid smoothly alongside and I immediately hopped on, taking a seat in first class where I hoped to arouse less suspicion. Surely anyone with something to hide was more likely to huddle in standard class, or between the cars.

I put my head back and pretended to be asleep but casually held my passport open in my lap. Perhaps if guards saw me they might assume I was just a strange tourist on an intercontinental journey, rather than the scruffy vagrant I really was. I considered pretending to be unwell; if questioned, at least my appearance gave such claims legitimacy.

All these thoughts swirled around my head throughout the tense crossing, until we serenely rolled into Cologne. The relaxed, almost inattentive approach towards security that I'd witnessed on all my stolen journeys would be impossible now, but at the time, I was enormously grateful for it. I was a few days from my twentieth birthday and had just arrived in a brand new, beautiful metropolis, crackling with energy in the morning rush hour.

The change was very welcome, but I remained homeless and hungry. No new scenery, however pretty, was likely to offer a magical transformation of my fortunes.

5

LOWS
AND HIGHS

The Cologne Hauptbahnhof, or main train station, was a maze of corridors and staircases. I spent my first few minutes in Germany scouting around the building for quiet nooks where I might be able to spend the nights ahead. Plenty of options arose, but all were very busy and I failed to find anywhere uninterrupted sleep seemed likely. Perhaps I'd be allowed to rest, unmolested by passengers and staff, but the police might be a lot more aggressive than in Amsterdam. I'd have to give it a shot and see.

I walked out of the building to catch my first glimpse of chilly Cologne, but the first thing to hit me was an intense aroma coming from a kiosk by the taxi rank. I moved closer and saw an old man serving deep-fried potato waffles, swimming in a pool of oil, for only one deutschmark. I'd never seen anything that looked so repulsive and unhealthy yet, more than anything, I craved to sample this delicious-smelling guilty pleasure. I dejectedly slunk off, annoyed that even such a small treat was denied me.

A charity collection bin received the last of my cents, useless as they were in this new city, and I set off to see what I could find. I had a fix on the station, so my next aim was to locate a gay bar and then perhaps the Salvation Army. In such an open and tolerant city, the former wasn't difficult to find but the latter proved another matter.

After consulting a couple of information maps, I found the name I wanted and started towards it. A longer walk ensued than I'd anticipated, but I finally arrived late morning. Then I turned straight back round to head back.

I'd spent two hours to reach an enrolment centre for the Territorial Army. I laughed at my own stupidity, which at least helped temper my annoyance. My grasp of German was limited, but I should have asked for directions rather than trying to make my own way into the suburbs. This was a minor irritation compared to other stuff I'd gone through, and I was glad to realise my spark of self-ridicule had never gone out. If I ever take myself too seriously, I'll know I'm in trouble!

I was terribly hungry and in quite a bad way, but made my way back to the bar I'd seen. It was on a street corner in a busy, upmarket shopping district. There were only a few people inside, not enough to guarantee my melting into the crowd. I had no way of buying a drink, but I caught the eye of who I guessed to be the manager behind the bar and he came over to the doorway.

I ventured to speak in my broken German, but he stopped

me at once with a kindly smile and indicated he could easily continue in English. My only advantage was to be born in the home country of a universal language!

I asked him if he knew of a hostel or homeless shelter nearby. Although he didn't, he asked me if I was okay. I nodded, but in a manner that made it apparent I was anything but. He invited me in, sat me at a table in the corner and brought over the acknowledged panacea for all English people: a hot cup of tea.

We talked and he introduced himself as Arthur Koenen. He was in his mid-twenties and worked in the bar for fun, while managing a hotel opposite the famous Gothic cathedral. It was a revelation to be with someone who genuinely cared enough to listen and to allow me a respite from the cold. His shift finished mid-afternoon. I thanked him for his time and made to leave. But the words that came next out of his mouth absolutely shocked me.

I was naïvely hoping, but hardly expecting, that he'd invite me back for the night, and he did – in a manner of speaking. He actually asked if I wanted to live with him. Gobsmacked is the best way to describe my reaction. I mumbled thanks for such a kind offer, though I couldn't possibly accept.

But he pressed the issue and eventually – because I liked him and found him attractive, but also because of the complete absence of other options – I agreed. He offered to buy dinner first, but I immediately countered with an alternative suggestion. Shortly afterwards, we were at the waffle stand, and I wolfed down several paper plates of the oil-soaked snacks. I felt guilty, disgusted and delighted all at the same time.

(I was so saddened when, on a return trip in 1998, I discovered the concourse had been redeveloped and the kiosk was no more.)

Arthur was a lovely man who fell in love with me all too quickly. He had a large duplex apartment in a peaceful suburb, and I started to fall for him too. Over the course of the next few weeks we grew close, and I began to cautiously settle into a life of domesticity.

This was my first real experience of sleeping with someone for whom I felt genuine affection. I tried to stay awake as long as I could while Arthur slept and I cuddled him. I've always believed that pleasantly novel experiences should be savoured in the moment and held onto in the future. The feeling of holding this person who was happy to be there in my arms was, to that point, startlingly unique for me. I never got used to the joy of waking up and seeing him beside me, or hearing him already in the kitchen, making coffee.

He had a few little toy hedgehogs on the bedroom window-sill, and we steadily added to their number. I had no job or income but spent my time lounging around, enjoying the extravagance of being indoors. I learnt German, which was always going to be the first step to integrating into my new country, and achieved proficiency in a very short time.

Inspired by our collection, I also became concerned by the welfare of the local hedgehogs and was distressed when I saw them dead in the street. At several junctions there were compact garden areas, often with concrete Ping-Pong tables, so I offered my help. With a few other residents, we built a hedgehog tunnel from one garden to another and it worked well.

(I'm delighted to say this passion continued, and in 2014 I became a patron of the British Hedgehog Preservation Society. Animal welfare has always been important to me and, although I'm not vegan, I don't wear leather and I'm fastidious about checking the ingredient lists on food. I also sorely wish that I could have a pet, but I'm at home so rarely that it's just not feasible.)

Living in Cologne was enjoyable and Arthur was just wonderful. He was kind, patient and utterly devoted. I, on the other hand, was a nightmare and a complete bastard. Fortunately, Arthur and I are now on good terms, chatting regularly and visiting each other's homes. I've apologised profusely to him and he has, as ever, both graciously accepted and lovingly understood. This is an enviable capacity that I'm simply incapable of, but Arthur can be lovingly content with anything. For all the time I was with him he only got angry once, and that was my fault as I was behaving like a horrible, spoiled brat.

I'm sorry to say I repaid his kindness with hurt. I invented the illusion that he was bound to throw me out, so I almost pre-empted it by forcing him do so. That, however, sounds like a mightily convenient excuse to justify my being a nasty piece of work. Here was a lovely person who had done nothing but care for me, and I was dismissive and disrespectful. How he even put up with me for a few months is beyond me, but the fact that he did is testament to the beautiful man he is. That he should accept my apology and we should remain friends is staggering.

I would pick rows with him for no reason, or assert some imagined moral or intellectual superiority just to insult him. I was obsessed with trying to dominate, rather than coexisting equally as partners. My behaviour was unforgivable, but he inexplicably continued to treat me with love and esteem. He bought me clothes, fed me, helped me fit into German life and was an absolute angel. I think all I gave him in return was to introduce him to a selection of English sitcoms – hardly a fair exchange.

After I started yet another pointless argument and stormed out petulantly, Arthur took the only course open to him and changed the locks. Now, I definitely don't blame him for this draconian act and in his position would have done the same – probably much sooner. However, at the time I was livid and couldn't see why he was taking such an unreasonable course of action. I acted out a final pitiful tantrum in the corridor, but ultimately slouched back off to the lonely streets. I'd been a most despicable child and got exactly what I deserved.

As I made my way back to the city centre, I maintained the pretence of being furious with Arthur while fully aware it was entirely my fault. This wasn't the only time I'd be a brute to someone who loved me. Amazingly, however, the next occasion was tempered by so much genuine love from both sides that my personality flaws were overcome and eventually worn down. But even then, this process would take many years...

Thanks to Arthur, the change in my appearance was considerable and I presented a healthy, reasonably handsome figure in decent clothes. I had a little money so I sought out another bar. I went in, bought a drink and waited for someone to talk to me. Unintentionally, my face must have matched my mood as everyone gave me a wide berth.

I knew Cologne, like most other large European cities, had a night sauna and I hadn't the fortitude to face a night at the train station. I'd foolishly expected that part of my life to be a thing of the past but failed to factor in my own pig-headed viciousness. I found it about fifty metres from where Arthur and I had first met, and spent the night there. It wasn't anywhere near the same standard as Amsterdam, and I was even happy to leave in the morning.

Here I was, alone and homeless anew in a place I was barely familiar with. I'd spent most of my time with Arthur indoors, just relishing the experience and avoiding other people. In retrospect this was probably wise, as my behaviour towards someone who loved me didn't bode well for how I'd treat anyone else.

It was warm so there were no immediate concerns about the weather, but the money inevitably ran out and I was back to my predictable state. I couldn't feel upset or bitter this time, as I'd had everything I'd ever wanted and thrown it all away. I'd been a total prat, and was now contemplating a life languishing once more at the very bottom.

At least I was dressed respectably and would hopefully avoid too much negative attention, so I spent the next two nights in the train station. However, sleep was very hard to come by due to the masses of people, and I doubt I convinced anyone in my weak charade as a tourist innocently waiting for a train.

It was Friday and I naïvely thought that if it had happened once, lightning might strike twice. I hung around outside another bar as the lunchtime rush was beginning. My last meal had been half a week ago, so I had to give this last frantic effort a try. But my labours proved fruitless and eventually I half-collapsed onto the pavement, cursing the staring eyes.

I was fragile and starving but the overwhelming sensation was anger at myself. I'm sure begging Arthur to take me back would have worked, as he was always so considerate, but he deserved so much more and I refused to subject him to any more pain.

Evening came and my thoughts unenthusiastically turned to the train station. The weekend crowds would be descending, but perhaps I'd be able to find somewhere quieter towards the back. The potential solitude was balanced by the fact it would be in the open air, so much colder, but I decided to at least give it a crack. Then I had the most unexpected and bizarre encounter of my whole life.

A man was leaning over me, offering his help. He was tall, in his fifties with short, cropped, greying hair, dressed smartly in black with a pleasant face and lyrical voice. I politely declined, smiled sadly, put my head down and waited for him to leave. He didn't budge and continued speaking, but I had to ask him to slow down, as my German wasn't up to full-speed fluency.

He instantly switched to flawless English but this no longer surprised me. Our European counterparts always so much more willing to learn our language than we theirs. He asked me if I'd ever thought of doing any modelling, and I gently laughed at his attempts to mock me. There was little he could say that I didn't deserve, or that would make me feel any worse.

Finally, the penny dropped as to what I thought he was

really after, but at least it would be a bed for the night. He introduced himself as Rainer Wackers, informing me he ran a modelling agency in Düsseldorf. He gave me his card, which appeared legitimate, though I still thought he was just trying to pick me up with an exotic back story.

I waited with a smirk for him to suggest discussing it further back at his place, but instead he pulled out his wallet and gave me a 100 DM note. If I was interested in a job, I should be at his office on Monday morning. He pointed to the address on the card, indicating the money would pay for my train fare and make the time until then more bearable. If I bothered to turn up, he'd consider the cash a loan against my first job; if not, it was a gift with his kind wishes.

He looked at me for a few moments and then wordlessly walked away, leaving me astonished. I gawped blankly at the bewildering gifts in my hands. My brain woke up and, without delay, I memorised the office's address just in case I lost the card.

I bought sandwiches and chocolate but saved half as a precaution, heading back to the night sauna. Paranoia had been a more constant companion than optimism, and I couldn't shake the idea that it was all a big con. My thoughts whirled into visions of the white slave trade and organised crime, so I decided to sleep on it. The sauna was busy, which would normally be most stimulating, but my libido was stubbornly stuck at zero. I showered and steamed before finding a secluded cabin and securely locking the door.

The next day I'd pretty much made up my mind to take Rainer up on his offer, but wanted the assurance of a little research first. But I was hindered by the weekend closures and it crossed my mind that, if a gang wanted to find people to exploit, then Friday night was the perfect time to do so. This was before the omniscient beast that is the internet, so I opted to try the local library and town hall.

Naturally, both were shut. I rang Arthur to check if he had any idea about it, but also to share the news and concur with him that he was quite right to kick me out. It was a cautious bid to mend bridges, as what I really wanted was for him to take me back.

I waited nervously but was directed straight to his answering machine. He may have been screening his calls, but I did leave a garbled message, partly in apology, partly giving details of where I was going – just in case. I understood that there was no way Arthur could pre-empt it if I was in trouble, but at least my destination was on record.

As a last resort, I consulted the Hauptbahnhof information stand. Fortunately, the lady there had directories covering several nearby cities. She opened that for Düsseldorf and quickly found the listing of the agency. Everything gave the impression of being above board, and I could always carefully check out the building on Monday. It all seemed too good to be true – and even that worried me.

The hours passed interminably slowly as I waited, with growing optimism, to commence the short journey. I'd been as frugal as possible, so by the time I bought my ticket on Monday morning, I still had half the money Rainer gave me.

I was on the train for less than half an hour, and arrived in Düsseldorf shortly after 8am in the middle of the heaviest hailstorm I'd ever seen. People were scurrying about or huddling determinedly under umbrellas to avoid the assault from the skies. I stared out into the white sheet as it was pelting down, crossed my fingers and turned to survey the city roadmap. My heart sank as I located the street, clear across the other side of the city centre. Having seen me at my worst, I predicted Rainer wouldn't be that bothered if I turned up drenched and bruised, so I planned out my route and made a run for it.

I predictably got lost, but arrived after a soggy, painful hour before the hail mercifully abated. I was very impressed by the modern smoked-glass-and-metal exterior, and then realised I was looking at the wrong building. I actually wanted next door, which had a respectable older façade.

With a degree of trepidation I found the bell and pressed. With no reply, the door unsettlingly buzzed open. I'd expected a receptionist to answer and my misgivings came flooding back. I observed the perfectly normal door latch as I went in, calculating that leaving in a hurry wouldn't be difficult if required. Holding the ornate bannister, I walked up two wide flights of stairs past other businesses and entered the office.

My first reaction was immense relief; it really was nothing more than a modelling agency. The walls were adorned with obligatory black and white photos, although every available surface was festooned with a variety of pot plants. The young man at the desk looked up and smiled, and I started to explain why I was there. But he'd been briefed and I was expected. Accepting a coffee, I made to sit down on the large sofa, only for Rainer to materialise instantly.

We spoke for a long time, mainly because I was so incredulous, and he was taking his time to calm my fears. I would be contracted to the agency, starting with a six-month term and subject to renewal afterwards. I'd be housed in Düsseldorf with a few other young men on his books, the negligible costs deducted from our earnings.

I was immediately on guard and suspected this was a clause to keep me imprisoned, but Rainer assured me I could leave any time I wanted – without obligation and with all conditions set out in writing. My perpetually pessimistic outlook was being challenged by the advent of a life-changing opportunity.

Rainer was thoroughly professional and probably used to this kind of reaction, but I could see his polite patience ebbing away as work waited. I gratefully accepted, shook his hand and signed the proffered contract. As I rose, he asked me if there was anything he could do for me to make my new life more contented. This required no reflection and the answer came immediately to my lips.

He was surprised when I said I wanted to legally change my name, but listened with interest as I detailed what I'd been told at the British Embassy in Amsterdam. He agreed to help later in the week, once I was settled in. Dispelling any lingering qualms, he also suggested delaying the signing. In the meantime, I'd be introduced to everyone with my brand new name, with which I could sign the contract. This raised the unanticipated but enjoyable issue of having to devise a new signature!

At that moment, CJ de Mooi was born and my new life genuinely began.

The house I moved into was agreeable enough, but small even for the five guys who were there prior to my squeezing in. Nevertheless, we were all in the same situation and we made do. There were three Germans, one Dutch and one Swiss, and all but one of us were gay. Any inhibitions about living in close quarters – including nudity, bathroom habits and sex – were quickly dismissed, as it would have been impossible to coexist otherwise.

There were three bedrooms so we all doubled up, but if anyone had company for the night the evictee would pile in with someone else. This really only happened when the straight boy – who was as relaxed as any of us – brought a girl back, as the other guys were usually quite content to make their own fun together.

But difficulties unavoidably arose, the most regular bone of contention being cleaning. One of the boys smoked, which caused more than a few disagreements, especially with me. I loathe smoking and can't stand anyone doing it near me. Why should I be forced to breathe someone else's poison?

Pots and pans would pile up in the sink, matched only by protests vehemently insisting it was someone else's turn to wash them. However, I spent a largely happy year and a half in the house. As it was somewhat of an improvement on my previous abode, I didn't complain too much.

It was a month later than intended, but Rainer kept his promise to travel with me to Bonn to change my name. I'd had a few low-key assignments and had been paid accordingly. It was then made quite clear that, from now on, I'd have to pay my own way. The loan and accommodation were immediately taken out of my salary, and I was left with a passable amount that would increase as I worked more consistently.

Reunification of Germany was underway but, for the moment, the British Embassy remained in the western capital. The deed poll itself wasn't particularly expensive, but associated costs soon added up. This single day might clear me out, but it was too critical to postpone as I'd been waiting for this day for many years.

I'd been thinking about my forename and, although I liked CJ, which was how I wanted to be addressed, I needed to select actual names to go with the letters. I plumped for Connagh Joseph because the spelling was slightly out of left field, which charmed me, and it also sounded nice. I couldn't believe how much I was looking forward to literally becoming my own man.

On arrival at the office, we were presented with a series of forms and instructions. I filled in the paperwork, presented photographs and my passport, declared the change wasn't for any criminal or fraudulent purposes, and waited for the checks. For his part, Rainer, as a professional person, stated that I was of noble character, which he was taking entirely on trust.

I would always be indebted to him for this, and of course for taking me off the streets in the first place. So I stayed with him for my entire modelling career. I attracted other, more lucrative contract offers during my time, but I was happy with him and my loyalty was my repayment.

After a surprisingly short wait, I was told everything was in place and processing was in motion. I braced myself to hear the wait time until I could collect my new passport and identity, anticipating it'd be at least a month. Even when the man said it would be at lunchtime, my old prejudices about bureaucracy kicked in. They were about to close for a ridiculously long break and anything we were paying for would have to wait. This, though, was Germany, and he advised us to go and get something to eat and return in two hours, when my documents would be ready.

I was astounded, and even Rainer raised an eyebrow at this welcome burst of efficiency. At the instructed time, I had a brand new passport in my hands and opened it to the photo page at the back. There, in official print, was my brand new name and I just stared at it in a state of pure euphoria. Rainer smiled alongside me, but we were both eager to get back to the office – him to work and me to sign my contract. He squealed when I caught him in an enormous hug, and then we started back.

The upshot of penning my new signature was being paid to walk up and down wearing nice clothes, or sitting in front of a camera, maybe in fewer clothes. I fell in love with Germany but may have a slightly distorted impression of it, as Cologne and Düsseldorf are very diverse and tolerant cities. I visited Berlin a couple of times but didn't really like it to be honest. But after reunification it became the world's busiest building site, as investment poured in, and I suppose I should give it another chance.

The highlights of my career were two occasions working with Claudia Schiffer. In 2001, I would be a contestant on *Wipeout* with the wonderful Bob Monkhouse. He was the kindest, most professional host I'd ever met, although another would claim that crown eight years later. He was the consummate professional, and it really upset me when he died.

As these shows encourage you to, I had a funny story to tell and related how, during one fashion show, Claudia and I noticed we had matching luggage cases. We finished our work and went our separate ways but, on arriving home, I opened the case to find I had all her personal possessions, including some clothing and underwear. It was all very funny and raised a hearty laugh from dear old Bob.

'Did you make use of any of the clothes?' he quipped.

I just laughed along with him realising in the nick of time how it might sound if I said I'd tried them on for size.

It was a great anecdote but, of course, completely made up. I knew how to play the television game and this memorable story helped get me on the programme. Nobody cared whether it was true or not – except, perhaps, Ms Schiffer, but I'm not aware she was an avid *Wipeout* viewer.

I travelled a little for work, including one wonderful week in San Francisco. I went with a boy called Duncan, although the night we got there the hotel had given away our room. We hardly cared and spent the whole evening flitting between bars and all-night diners, including the amazing Baghdad Café. I was immediately taken with this city, especially its legendary openness towards gay people. This was especially evident in the Castro district, which we wandered around agog during our free time. Mostly, however, I did runway work in western Europe, which was engaging but lacking in any kind of challenge.

I left the models' house and rented a tiny flat in Cologne for my last three years with the agency. I adored having my own front door and even – shock horror – started to acquire a social life. As I went to bars, my face became familiar and I slowly attracted friends. I had hoped to find love but this never happened, and I constantly toyed with trying to rekindle things with Arthur.

There was no denying I'd changed. My anger and inherent hostility had mellowed, but I came to realise our history would be too much of a burden and knew I had to let things be. Even now, I've never managed to forgive myself for what I ruined.

I fell into an amiable cycle of bars, clubs and saunas, but it was futile to expect anything other than anonymous sex in any of these, and I needed more. I'd give a man my number and end up waiting impatiently by a silent telephone. I honestly lost count of how often I arranged a meeting only to be stood up. I'm sure most weren't intended as malicious rejections, but after a few dozen, I did develop a complex!

Perhaps my inability to find a relationship caused my wanderlust to surface once more. It was 1994; I was in my mid-twenties with a reasonable nest egg of money saved up, but lacking direction or ambition for the future. Of course, my acting aspirations bubbled under the surface, but the cold, hard light of reality suppressed them. Dreams are all very well, but if they're unachievable then surely they'll just gnaw away at your spirit.

I agonised over it for weeks but finally concluded to leave the agency and move. I'd loved Amsterdam even when my conditions had been terrible, so I wanted to see it from the other side. I could afford to live there for a while, so I went to see Rainer. We went out for a final goodbye dinner at a local Italian restaurant that we both enjoyed. Without thinking, I'd actually expected him to pay, but when the bill arrived he correctly insisted we split it. This was the way he'd always acted, and I respected and loved him for it. I mumbled my thanks and we hugged for ages, before I returned to my flat to finish packing.

I didn't have much even after nearly five years, and a lot of what there was, including books and ornaments, either stayed in the flat or went to charity shops. I fitted my life into two shoulder bags and headed to the train station. Germany had been so good to me, and I truly regretted leaving, but the time was right.

I'd been back to Amsterdam once or twice in the intervening years, but it felt very odd to return with the intention of living there legitimately. I'd arranged a flat share with a friendly chap called Tom who lived in Osdorp, a suburb on tram route number one. I'd assumed this meant it was very close to the city centre, but I was fantastically wrong, as it was about four miles south. This required either a seventy-minute walk or half-hour tram journey. I usually preferred the former, as fitness is important to me. I only acquiesced if it was later at night or, in the case of the night sauna, stupidly early in the morning. It was fine for the time being though, and Tom was away with his husband most of the time.

I'm not one for sentimentality, but top of my list was to return to the station and look for a rough sleeper. I wanted someone in real need, not like the one who was abusive to me all those years earlier. I found a young girl, no more than eighteen, crouched at the base of a pillar behind the ticket hall. After a short chat, she revealed she'd run away after a big fight with her stepfather. I bought her some food and offered to take her to Leger des Heils. She thanked me but refused, so I pushed a few notes into her hand and left. I sincerely hoped she'd return home and find a resolution but, based on my own experiences, my optimism wasn't high.

Although I had my savings, I wanted to get a job, as this would give my stay a more permanent status. I was young, fit, intelligent and not hideous to behold, so I hoped to find exciting and invigorating employment. I hunted around but my single offer came from one of the biggest nightclubs in the city. The Roxy on the Singel was a huge, gaudy club over many floors, with a welcoming and fully inclusive reputation. This sounds mightily impressive until you learn my job was washing dishes.

Don't get me wrong – like so many other occupations, this is a vital role and I have nothing but respect for those who do it. I, however, didn't fall in love with it, especially after my glamorous years in Germany, and lasted barely six months. The solitary advantage was the money. My salary was pretty good and cash in hand, so I didn't pay tax. I justified this by arguing that I took nothing else out of the Dutch system and paid my own way in everything. I was giving far more to the economy than it was losing through my minor avoidance. That failed to alter the fact that six nights a week, often until sunrise, I was getting my hands very dirty scrubbing other people's filthy dishes. It enabled me to live in a city I adored, but it hardly represented a very fulfilling course.

Painfully slowly, I began to learn the extraordinarily difficult Dutch language. There are so many sounds that simply don't exist in English, and already knowing German proved a significant hindrance. I had a wonderful realisation after about two years in Düsseldorf, when it suddenly occurred that I'd been thinking in German. I hadn't translated it back and forth in my head; I could actually think in this new tongue. I remember giggling manically at the time, but I'd never succeed at that unconscious level in Dutch.

Often I'd start speaking a sentence in Dutch but involuntarily switch to German halfway through. I must have caused a lot of amusement, or confusion, before I gained enough proficiency to speak without deliberate attention. I've always found languages quite easy to pick up, but there's no substitute for being surrounded by native speakers. Communication is so visual, even if some of the words are lost on you; facial expressions, hand gestures or intonation are all useful tools for translation.

Now I rarely speak German, so if someone tries to engage me, I'll be stuttering and hesitant. However, whenever I'm back in Cologne, within a day or two I'm wittering on as freely as I ever did. It's forever buried in there and requires the slightest encouragement to be coaxed out. Total immersion in a native language is, without question, the best way to learn it.

My love for Amsterdam was as strong as ever and the bond endures to this day. I return twice a year, taking different friends to introduce them to its delights in the certainty that they'll see the city through my eyes. After nearly a year though, the inevitable restlessness kicked in once more. I'd given up my job at the Roxy and was running low on funds. I couldn't afford to move into the city proper without fulltime employment, and was feeling in the way at the flat, as I think Tom wanted his husband to move in.

It was autumn 1995 and I started to seriously contemplate

a previously unconscionable move back to Britain. I was by no means unhappy in Holland, but had the impression that my time there had run its course. By no means did I consider the country of my birth to be my home, but another change of surroundings, this time without the rigours of learning another language, was attractive.

I made my decision far too quickly, just upping and leaving. Spontaneity has been a gift I've always cherished, but this was the most stupid thing I'd done in a very long time. I reversed the route that had carried me to Amsterdam for the first time, via the Hook of Holland and Harwich, and settled in for the journey. My giddy impetuosity lasted until the train was trundling the final few miles to Liverpool Street station, when it suddenly dawned on me that I had nowhere to stay in London. I hadn't stepped foot in this alien land for seven years, and had even rejected modelling work here when it had been offered.

I'd calculated I had sufficient money to cover me for three months, but my usual fastidious planning had gone awry. I'd based my calculations on rent figures in Amsterdam, not hotel prices in London. At the latter rate, I'd be broke in a week, so I had to make arrangements damn quickly.

I caught the tube to Embankment, intending to pop up to Soho and call the Gay Switchboard for information on flat shares. I walked back above ground and was horrified to be confronted by countless homeless people. They were living and sleeping rough, begging or hanging around the park waiting for nightfall, as I'd done on so many long, empty days.

I can't say what I'd expected but nothing at all had

changed while I'd been away. It was beyond belief that any government permitted this to continue at the end of the twentieth century in one of the world's great cities. I carried my bags through the crowds, trying not to look at those holding out their hands, desperately trying to catch an eye or tug at a heartstring. I'd been in their terrible predicament for so long, but here I was trying – along with all the other commuters, and the government – to pretend they were invisible. I don't think I've ever despised myself more than I did at that moment.

I called the switchboard and was given a handful of leads. I had to take refuge in one of the least foul, but still stinking, phone boxes and call round the numbers, scribbling details down with pen and paper. We forget how inconvenient pre-internet life was; oh, how we suffered until smartphones saved us!

I made appointments for the next day, after opting for a cheap hotel that night. I went to view various flat shares but there was nothing that appealed. Most were just out to make a quick buck, offering as little as they could in return. I think I offended one woman as soon as she opened the door (not that I cared in the slightest). I was instantly bombarded by a wave of stale cigarette smoke, so I made a hurried excuse to get out.

I found a small room at a flat in New Cross in south London. It wasn't great, but I needed a temporary refuge and base from which to make my future plans. Unfortunately, after only a few days there, the flaws in this plan were made terrifyingly clear.

One midweek evening I was travelling on the bus into

the city centre. My favourite bar, Brief Encounter just off Trafalgar Square, was the destination. We passed through Elephant and Castle, an area regrettably noted for its violence and racial tension. A gang (there's no other word for it) of five black teenage boys got on and started shouting at the passengers. I moved to get off the bus but this made the mood instantly more threatening. Perhaps I should have been alert to it, as nobody else moved a muscle, but I saw no reason to put up with such crude and intimidating behaviour.

Straight away I was bombarded with homophobic and racist taunts. One boy boasted loudly that, if he saw me again, he'd cut my throat. The eyes of every other person on the bus stared resolutely, unseeingly in front of them, but I had no doubt that, if I was attacked, someone would offer assistance. I was very stupid to believe this.

The doors opened and I began to step off, but then I felt a heavy blow on the back of my head. I fell face-first onto the pavement, and was immediately kicked in the head and stomach as they crowded around me. They punched, kicked and spat at me for several minutes, all the time screaming the vilest abuse.

Despite it being a busy urban area in transport Zone One of London, not a single person stopped to help. When it was finally over and the gang had slunk off giggling, I was left literally black and blue in a pool of blood. An elderly lady came over to give me a tissue, and that was the sole instance of human kindness I experienced. Many pairs of eyes had watched the onslaught, but no pair of hands was moved to do anything about it. After years amongst caring communities abroad, this was an awful shock.

I may be a liberal, but I don't pretend I can forgive any of this. Decrying their lack of opportunities and pointing to deprived circumstances is no justification. These thugs can't blame anyone else but themselves for their violence. I truly hope, and expect, that these pieces of filth are now rotting in prison.

I got to Soho and tried to clean myself up. I looked a complete mess and my clothes were spattered red. One guy asked me what had happened as I was obviously close to tears, but, incredibly, he just shrugged when I told him. I couldn't believe this blasé attitude. Was it so expected for gay people to be physically attacked that nobody considered it worthy of compassion? I couldn't spend long in the bar, and with no friends I felt lonelier than ever. As new and as strange as it was, the room in New Cross was my only sanctuary and I hurried to return.

After leaving the West End, I was on the same bus route back when the gang got on again at Elephant and Castle. Our eyes instantly met, and they all smiled menacingly, saying they'd be getting off at the same stop as me. As they climbed the stairs, I went straight to the driver and asked him to call the police. He sneered at me, telling me to sit down and shut up.

As calmly as I was able, I told him I'd been attacked by a gang armed with knives, and that if he didn't make the call I'd report the incident and make sure the bus company found out. His job meant more to him than the welfare of his passengers, so he morosely did what I asked and sunk back into his seat, refusing to look at me.

Two policemen appeared unexpectedly soon, and gestured

for me to get off. I thanked the driver, but he growled an expletive and drove off.

The officers asked me why I was threatening a driver and holding up the bus service. I stared at them until it dawned on me they were not responding to the call. They'd just seen this guy standing at the front of a bus which was stationary, and assumed I'd done something wrong.

I explained everything and, to my horror, they just laughed. I stood there covered in blood, showing blatant evidence of an attack, and these cretins weren't going to do a damn thing about it. It could be that they were trying to hide their embarrassment at misunderstanding the situation, or that – far more likely – they couldn't have cared less. I pleaded with them to make a report, but they turned away. I shouted at them to come back.

'Keep it up and you'll be arrested, kid,' said one in a mocking tone. 'You got just what you deserved. Don't be a homo!'

'Fine, arrest me! That way I can make an official report about the attack and your language!' I screamed, making sure that the crowd around me heard.

This forthright approach visibly shook him, but he just turned his back and walked off. I noted his number and the next day, ensuring I was still in my bloodied clothes, I made a report at the local station. I left my details, but hardly surprisingly, I heard nothing more.

There are, of course, many members of the police services around this country who are diligent, caring and hard working. Then there are others who are corrupt, heartless and lazy. All too often we hear terms such as 'institutionally racist', 'homophobic' and 'sexist' applied to the police and, as many enquiries attest, they turn out to be accurate. Such experiences are enough to totally eradicate any trust whatsoever.

This whole horrible experience added to the considerable unease I already felt about settling in this country. After thinking about it for a couple of weeks, while my bruises were healing, I concluded that as long as I was on the move, I wouldn't put down roots. So, I decided to spend some time travelling around, which I could justify to myself as nothing more than an extended holiday. It was a great shame I didn't take longer, as it might have provided some badly needed British geographical knowledge for *Eggheads*!

I spent time in Brighton, Manchester, Liverpool, Glasgow and Edinburgh. I liked Scotland, but the place I was immediately attracted to was Liverpool. There was a sense of glories past, and its spectacular architecture and history inspired me. The population also shared a collective electric energy that I adored.

I volunteered for the HIV charity Body Positive and stayed in the city for several months, far longer than intended. Of course, I eventually pushed on to pastures new but later wondered if this was because I'd made a couple of friends. Had I really become so fearful of people getting close that, at the first sign of intimacy, I literally ran scared?

This worried me but rather than be maturely seeking to advance relationships beyond a superficial level, I chose to avoid friends at all costs. To describe this as a self-defence mechanism would be foolhardy. I was just being idiotic, whispering to myself – as so many had loudly shouted at me in the past – that I was worthless and that nobody would ever really want to know me.

Brighton was a revelation, however, and I enjoyed my stay there immensely. The two reasons it is ingrained in my consciousness are almost diametrically opposed: Brighton was where I first joined a gym, and I very quickly became addicted to training. Being a convenient ten minutes' walk from where I stayed was a bonus, and I often made three visits a day. I've never been interested in muscular or athletic bodies, but plenty of gay men are and I attracted a considerable amount of new attention, which was nice.

The other aspect may have been a consequence of this: I contracted syphilis. In the modern world this is no longer such a life-threatening problem but the treatment was horrendous. Twice a day for seventeen days, I went to the hospital and had an injection in each buttock. That's sixty-eight in total. Each injection involved a very large syringe full of what was essentially thick liquid metal. Due to its size and consistency, each took twenty minutes and, for hours afterwards, I felt like I'd been kicked very hard in each cheek. It was completely effective, but if ever a cure was worse than the disease, this was it.

I'd gained no real satisfaction from just over a year wandering around, and found myself back in London with the same lack of ambition and interest. My money was, as always, on the verge of petering out, and I couldn't waste it on accommodation. So I returned to my old ways, spending nearly a month sleeping in the small church courtyard at the end of Old Compton Street, along with a depressingly large number of other people. I was very disappointed to see, shortly afterwards, that this small oasis had been made inaccessible at night by very high, threatening railings. It was another example of society turning its back on those most in need, and it made my blood boil.

One evening, in search of distraction, I went into a bar and straightaway found myself looking into a familiar face. I'd briefly known Wendy from my previous period in London, as I'd met her friend Stephen once. Given the nature of transient friendships, we'd both lost touch with him, but here she was in another social circle. She chatted with me and soon revealed she was living in Fulham with her mother. They had a spare box room to rent; it wasn't up to much but I was welcome to it for a very nominal figure, if I didn't mind the clutter. I laughed and assured her I'd be able to cope. Fulham is a great location and how bad could a little clutter be?

The box room turned out to be more box than room. Mysterious cardboard packages were balanced precariously against walls and cases were scattered around the floor at random. I dared not look under the bed for fear of attack by the myriad of spare clothes that reached out like corpses from the darkness.

It was all coated in a generous helping of dog hair from the family pet, Scooter. Now, never had I seen such a demented creature as dear Scooter. I think he was a golden retriever, but whatever his breed, he was bat-crap crazy.

I've always been attracted to those of a quirky or unusual nature, rather like myself. I don't care whom you are or what you do, but if you're different from the norm that's cool by me. I became very attached to Scooter and, even though he was already well advanced in years, adored our long walks and energetic runs. When we returned to the house, he'd have his regular shake, depositing another thick layer of hair over my room and I, but I never really minded.

The house was warm and Wendy and her mother, Lily, were welcoming as only a West Indian family can be. Lily was a singer and Wendy, coincidentally, worked for a homeless charity. Unsurprisingly perhaps, she was forthcoming and kind towards me.

I needed a job and, although temporarily happy in my insular life, I knew the travel bug would soon reappear and so cash reserves were crucial. I applied to be a waiter in a five-star hotel opposite Kensington Palace. I had no experience – and, to be honest, no interest – in the job, but I bluffed my way through the interview and started work in November 1996. It paid well and was an easy walk from the house.

I was twenty-seven years old and only working to collect enough money to vanish abroad again. But then six months passed and, contrary to my intentions, my savings had gone down rather than up. I think I'd been sucked into the illusion of a steady income and home life, rather than remaining focused on my goal.

A promotion to bar manager reduced my workload to practically zero, as I rarely had more than a single customer an evening. I generally sat around fighting off encroaching boredom. To compensate for this, I was spending freely to provide some form of inspiration. I'd progressed well past the stage of finding bars or clubs enticing, but trips with Wendy to New York, nice clothes and other luxuries added up to me living considerably beyond my means. I was now working in order to live, the usual daily reality for the majority of sensible adults. But I was certainly far from sensible, so falling into such an unexpected trap alarmed me.

I remember spending Sunday, 4 May 1997 at work, and serving nobody for my entire afternoon shift. I walked back to the house and, as Wendy was already in bed, took Scooter for a late walk. Even then, the clock hadn't yet reached midnight, so I flopped down on the lounge sofa, switched on the television for a while and absently watched some programme or other. It may have been *Desmond's*, which I enjoyed at the time.

Now, you may think these details are not important, and in themselves they're not. Nevertheless, I would passionately love a clearer memory of that evening, because of what followed. The next day would herald the single most important event of my life.

6

LOVE CHANGES EVERYTHING

I was very much looking forward to the World Snooker Championships Final. Stephen Hendry had won twenty-nine straight matches at the Crucible and very few people, me included, doubted he'd win his thirtieth against the outsider Ken Doherty. With this victory and no brouhaha, he'd serenely sail to his sixth consecutive world title.

I've always been fascinated by snooker. I was three or maybe four when I saw a match on television, and distinctly remember that Eddie Charlton was playing. That in itself might be enough to put most people off the game for life, but I was enraptured by it. I can truthfully say that, of all the benefits my television and stage careers have brought me, becoming involved in the snooker scene and getting to know the players has been the most treasured. I can't, however, play the game and barely know which way round to hold the cue. But a memorable day was spent playing with Kirk Stevens on the Crucible match table, with the wonderful Michaela Tabb refereeing. Still, we'll get to my snooker obsession later – including an appearance on *Pointless Celebrities* with Shaun Murphy!

I had some time before the day's play began so I went for a stroll. It was a sunny bank holiday lunchtime, so where better to go than a cemetery? Why this should seem morbid or strange I really don't know. I've always found cemeteries alluring places; their treats and surprises include fantastic architecture and interesting graves hidden around corners, or under huge wild brambles.

To be honest though, I've never quite understood the whole concept of burial. Dropping a slab of rotting flesh in the ground, with a stone sticking out to indicate its location, baffles me. I can embrace the idea of open-air cremation or leaving a body on a mountaintop to feed animals, or be pecked away by birds. There's a sense of closing the circle, of returning to where we came from. At present, I don't care what happens to me, and I imagine I'll care even less after I'm dead. If I have a slight preference, it's to be left to medical science – but maybe that's so I can be the centre of attention just one last time.

Cemeteries are, of course, cruising and pickup joints. They tend to be frequented by a lot of gay men, but some (notably Highgate) are popular with absolutely everyone. This may come as a surprise to some but then, I guess, so do dogging sites. There's no point pretending these places don't exist or serve a public need. It's far better, in my opinion, to have a controlled, discreet environment rather than all manner of things happening in the street, frightening the horses.

A slow meander down North End Road out of Fulham, and a turn towards Earl's Court, brought me to Brompton Cemetery. This is a splendid, medium-sized public park next to Stamford Bridge football stadium, featuring a few notable interments such as Emmeline Pankhurst and Brian Glover. Viewers of Guy Ritchie's *Sherlock Holmes* will recognise the location of the scene where Lord Blackwood's grave is broken open. It was filmed on the central thoroughfare and the large circular area at its heart, and this is where I found myself as the clock chimed two.

I looked to the other side of the circle and saw two guys chatting away. One was wearing a baseball cap and the other a strangely heavy coat for such a warm day. He disappeared almost at once but the face beneath the cap turned to me and smiled. Summoning up what little nonchalance I could, I ambled over and said hello. His name was Andrew, and within five minutes we were on our way to his flat in South Kensington.

Once there, he introduced his lovely flatmate Sarah, who he'd met through work as they were both costume designers. She was a tall, slim designer with long, curly red hair, sharing a flat with a gay man – you need no longer wonder where the situation for *Will & Grace* came from!

After an exceedingly pleasant afternoon, we settled down to watch the final session of the snooker. Andrew sat on the sofa with me on the floor between his legs. He had categorically no interest in the game but tolerated it only to make me happy. I put my arm around his ankle, leaned against a big fluffy cushion and watched Ken Doherty pull off the most unexpected win to become world champion.

Many years later, I told Ken why this day had been so special for me too, for quite different reasons. He smiled and hugged me, and because of that he remains one of my very favourite players.

I spent the night with Andrew and woke early the next day, as he had to go to work. There followed the usual embarrassing pause when neither person wants to be the first to make a verbal commitment, but I was way beyond letting chances slip through my fingers. I asked if I could see him again, and the relief and happiness on his face didn't signify a refusal. Seventeen hours after we'd met, I was passionately and hopelessly in love.

We had a second night together and then he dropped the bombshell. In five weeks he was leaving for Zimbabwe until mid-November to work on a film; then, almost straight after, he planned to go travelling around South America for a further three months.

I was devastated but wanted to hold on to Andrew for whatever brief time I could. Getting hurt was unavoidable, but I could cherish the moments until then. I bit my tongue but soon burst out with a confession of love for him on the Wednesday. He reciprocated – although I noted the extra day it took him to do so.

I mindlessly continued with work, only thinking about the evenings with Andrew ahead. This continued for two weeks, but his departure and my emotional agony loomed large, until I was compelled to make a painful pronouncement. We discussed it and concurred that the best option was a clean and complete break. It would only break our hearts to become more deeply involved before he vanished for nearly a year.

The choice was made and we agreed not to see each other again. I would last a grand total of thirty-five hours.

I trust I don't strike anyone as a mushy, soppy person. Just because I'm gay doesn't automatically make me understanding, loving and tolerant – I hope I possess those qualities anyway, but it's got nothing to do with whom I'm attracted to. I'm surprised by the number of times straight friends ask for advice with their love lives, assuming my sexuality gives me special insights and a capacity for caring. Don't they know me at all?

Yet the next evening, I was suddenly transformed into a creature so sickeningly sweet and saccharin I'm surprised my teeth didn't instantly rot. I phoned Andrew and, in my most angelic tone (not something that comes naturally to me, you'll appreciate), asked, hypothetically, what would happen if I were to come over that night. I kept this toe-curling, twee procedure up for the entire week until he was worn down and finally relented.

If I had to survive with only his memory while he was away, so be it. We'd at least realised we were meant to be together.

At the end of May, less than four weeks after that wonderful day in Brompton Cemetery, we began flat hunting together. We found a very small place to rent overlooking Putney Green on the King's Road. It was the epitome of bland and beige, but, with both our names on the lease, I was optimistic it could be transformed into a real home.

A week later, Andrew left for the set in Zimbabwe. He was filming a big costume drama series there, and neither could nor wanted to get out of the commitment. He did, though, cancel his trip to South America so that we might start to build a life together on his return, and even arranged for me to visit him in Harare for the first two weeks of September.

I was very nervous for Andrew, as this was when Robert Mugabe was growing increasingly belligerent towards the white farmers in his country. This man is the archetype of a despotic tyrant, and his policy of driving farmers out – some of whom were murdered – so that their land could by seized by people with no idea what to do with it was an economic nightmare. Of course, he was insulated from the poverty and famine that the population endured all around him. I'm writing these words eighteen years on and the monster, incredibly, remains in power while poor Zimbabwe continues to suffer.

Tragically, this pattern continues around the planet, most noticeably in modern day Russia. After years of improvement and benefits following the collapse of the Soviet Union, the country is cursed with Vladimir Putin, a leader seemingly intent on returning it to the days of old. Minorities are abused, currencies fall, people die but those at the top simply don't care, shielded from the harsh realities and arrogantly dismissive of ineffectual international condemnation.

The thought of Andrew being in such an environment scared me, even if matters were not quite as terrible as they were to become. We spoke every day, helped by only a very slight time difference. He told me how his days were frantically progressing, and I moaned about the damp patch on the ceiling of the bedroom that had started as a mere spot and was now a metre in length. The landlord was doing nothing to attend to it, so we planned to move out when Andrew got back, citing health concerns.

(The landlord threatened us with legal action if we didn't pay the full year's rent. We invited her to go right ahead, and printed her letter – alongside the report we'd got from the council about the damp – in the local Kensington newspaper. She mumbled some retraction about a breakdown of communications, but still had the gall to ask me to show a prospective renter – who was expected to pay even more money – around the flat. She received a very short answer.)

Nothing much happened over the following weeks, except I handed in my notice. My work was unfulfilling and, although I know that's true of a lot of jobs, I don't have the discipline to put up with anything I don't like. My daily costs were low and Andrew's income covered the flat and expenses, so we managed.

I spent a lot of my time at the local gym, which was more than balanced by my ever-improving impersonation of a couch potato. The television stayed on most of the time from early morning until late at night, even though there was very little to interest me. I was due to visit Africa on 5 September, the day after my last shift at the hotel, and I was already counting down. This was my impatient mood when the television flickered into life on the morning of 31 August.

I stared at the screen through eyes that were still waking up, but couldn't grasp what I saw. There was a newsreader – perhaps Peter Sissons – in front of a large picture of Princess Diana with the dates 1961-1997 beneath it. Yes, I knew what year she was born and I knew what year it was now, so why was the BBC bothering to tell me?

I got up to make a coffee, vaguely listening to him droning on, but suddenly I bolted into the moment as my sluggish brain processed the words. I sat down, mug in hand, transfixed by the images. I didn't move for an hour, and even then it took the ringing of the phone to shake me free.

It was Andrew. Filming had been suspended so everyone there could watch the news too. We spoke slowly, bonded by a strange sadness at being apart and unable to personally share an unexpected grief for someone we didn't know. I'm certainly no royalist but Diana was a new, different kind of royal; perhaps this is why she resonated so deeply with the general public.

I'd followed her campaigning for those infected with HIV with special interest; her efforts to interact with those living with, or affected by, the disease massively transformed popular opinion and dispelled a stigma. Very few stories possess truly international appeal, but as the report flew around the world, it appeared every single item was discarded in favour of Diana's death.

Andrew and I felt relieved that we'd be physically together in less than a week, but I was, rather selfishly, dreading going into work. The hotel commanded direct views across Kensington Gardens and faced Kensington Palace full on. This was sure to be a focus of national grief over the coming days, but no one could have foreseen the outpouring to follow.

The flowers had already started to build up by the time I arrived, and the hotel remained uniformly quiet for the entire day. I was used to not serving anyone over a shift, but to not even catch sight of a single guest was spooky.

Five days dragged by, and the vast sea of bouquets and gifts outside the palace gates was ingrained into our collective consciousness. I wanted to be free of the place and its stifling atmosphere, and I don't just mean the hotel. London was literally funereal, almost waiting for the cathartic release of Diana's laying to rest.

The morning of my flight, the day before the actual service, I arrived at the airport four hours early, yearning for my escape. Never lacking in chutzpah, I casually asked at the airline check-in if any upgrades were available. I had an economy ticket but most carriers oversell the class and bump up selected passengers, so I thought I'd try my luck. One was apparently on offer and I was travelling alone, so it was easy to allocate it to me.

My long flight to Johannesburg would be in the comfort of first class. I had to call Andrew from the airport and tell him, but a connection from a public phone box to a mobile phone on another continent was not cheap. Nevertheless, it was worth it for the half-minute conversation. I frantically fed the slot with coins as the phone beeped hungrily throughout.

I don't remember much of the flight, and have no recollection of the connecting shuttle to Harare either. We landed just before midnight on a piece of overgrown tarmac by a corrugated-iron bomb shelter that was, allegedly, the terminal. Security was of no evident interest, as Andrew was right there at the bottom of the stairs leading off the plane. I've never seen a smile happier than his right then, and I hope he can say the same of mine. We'd been apart for three months but now, his work notwithstanding, we had two weeks together and were fully determined to enjoy them.

Predictably, that was easier said than done. Given the time

restrictions of location filming, Andrew was awake by 5am and didn't generally return until 11pm. This was his routine six days a week, so his solitary free day in the middle of my stay was destined to be our lone opportunity. I imagined he'd want a lie-in but no, nothing of the sort. Long before sunrise, we were already fifty miles north of Harare for a morning balloon flight and breakfast.

It was stunningly glorious as we watched the rays creep over the mountains in the distance, waving at farm workers below. This brought home another tragic reality of the modern world: every single person I met in Zimbabwe, without exception, was friendly, courteous and fully accepting of any other lifestyle or religion. They were all warm, wonderful souls, and I see this pattern replicated in country after country.

Most people just want themselves and others to be happy, living in peace and security. It's those in government – usually in bids to increase their own corrupt power and wealth – who forcefully influence the lives and opinions of the populace. I spent a while chatting to an old man begging in the doorway of a Harare department store. I gave him some money, and he repaid me with a look of disbelief that an affluent white man should even remotely care. But he was also generous with his time and unswervingly polite. This is what I've found wherever I've travelled, but it infuriates and upsets me. The minority, clinging to its powerbase, refuses to allow the majority to live in a spirit of love and respect.

After our wonderful flight, we went into the city and bought a silly little cuddly toy. It was a small white gorilla adorned with the nametag 'Mongo', clutching a red heart with the logo 'I Love You' upon it. A ridiculous little thing to be thrown in the bin as soon as the buyer regained his senses, eighteen years later Mongo sits proudly at the head of our bed. Andrew had a strange affect on me, and back then I wondered if I was truly beginning to mellow or even, improbably, become happy.

My time in Harare was usually spent racking up meagre expenses on the film company's account at the Sheraton, where everyone was staying. The daily breakfasts were copious and hugely varied; suitably bloated, I'd find a quiet sun lounger by the pool and settle down with a book. Occasionally, I'd ask one of the many waiters who floated around for a chilled bottle of cola and a grilled cheese sandwich: don't tell me I don't know how to live!

It was all very nice, but I told Andrew I was getting a little bored, and was looking forward to going home. He looked at me and smiled, and I realised what I'd said. For the first time in my life, I'd actually meant that particular, very loaded word: I no longer merely lived in a house; I had a home because it was shared, despite his temporary absence, with the man I loved.

I returned to London two days later, rather thankful to have missed all the insanity surrounding Diana's funeral. I'd been unable to avoid watching it on the news, mainly because there was virtually no other item receiving coverage. Andrew was to join me in six weeks and then we'd make a plan – *our* plan – for the future. I fell into bed, exhausted from the long return flight in economy class. I stared at the myriad colours in the expanding damp patch above my head, and hoped this wouldn't be the night it fell in.

Andrew's flight back was the redeye overnight, but I was there by 7am, hopping excitedly at the arrivals gate. He plodded through, tanned but visibly tired; I grabbed the collection of bags out of his hand, dropped them to the ground and wrapped my arms tightly around him.

Back at King's Road, we collapsed straight into bed to catch up on some badly needed sleep. He was furious about the wet stain on the ceiling, but I insisted he rest before an angry call to the landlord that afternoon. She sauntered around, more interested in the disembodied voices on her mobile. Fine, we decided; if that's the way she wants to do business, she's not getting any more of ours. We gave our notice, exchanged and publicised the subsequent letters and moved out.

We stayed with Wendy briefly, but this was unlikely to be anything other than a stopgap as Andrew is allergic to animal fur. With Scooter's amazing ability to shed his bodyweight every time he moved a muscle, the two were never going to be close companions.

We considered various options and, after I'd related my experiences from my time there, opted for Brighton. It was an easy commute to London for Andrew's work, possessed a relaxed atmosphere and was by the sea, which hugely appealed to us both. Over the next three and a half years, we actually lived twice in the city, once in neighbouring Hove and then again right in the heart of Brighton, overlooking the pavilion. This time though we were resolute to buy, as renting was an expensive option that left us at the mercy of a landlord or landlady's whims.

I say 'we' but of course I mean Andrew alone. I had no

Above left: Floating along during the 2015 London Marathon.

Above right: My first ever pantomime was *Dick Whittington* in Lincoln.

Below left: With the gorgeous Brenda Blethyn. She gives such lovely cuddles!

Below right: On the set of *Revenge of the Egghead*.

Above left: In full costume for *The International Stud*. I'm a little concerned about how good I look in drag!

Above right: The Stonewall Inn in New York, where Pride began.

Below: With Ed Theakston on the set of *The Renata Road* (we rarely took notice of the signs!).

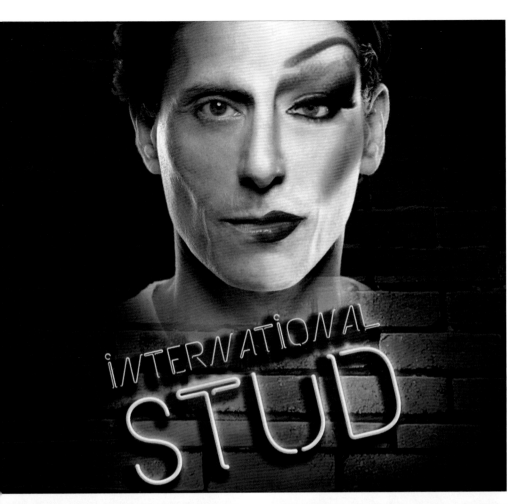

Above: Promotional image for *The International Stud* at the 2015 Edinburgh Fringe.

Below left: In a tense moment with Mike Cole during a performance of *Safe Sex*.

Below right: We each got a superhero picture for *Eggheads* (although I preferred the *Guardian* describing me as '...a future Bond villain.'

Above: With my best friend Dan in Amsterdam.

Below left: Trying to look moody but actually just struggling with the zip.

Below right: With Jamie at a *Big Issue* charity auction. He never forgave me for winning the star prize!

income at all, so all the responsibility was on him. He must have been pretty confident we were in it for the long run to make such an investment. I, however, wasn't so sure.

Mirroring my unforgivable behaviour with Arthur, I nearly brought it all crashing down. It's only because Andrew is such a deeply loving individual that we were able to get through it. Several times, I fell into my old, detestable habit of starting arguments for no reason.

I can reach a very intense, wrathful pitch when riled, although I was never really angry with Andrew. It may start as a piffling tiff over the most insignificant issue, but I was a sure-fire bet to massively overreact and blow it out of all proportion. But by now we'd been together for two years, which was – let me check, ah yes – almost two years longer than my earliest serious involvement.

I'd met Klaus Sorenson the day before my twenty-first birthday. He was a model at the agency and it didn't take much to see why. He was Danish, tall, slim, blond, blue eyed and drop-dead gorgeous. We immediately fell for each other but, to this day, I can't imagine what he, who could have had anyone at all, saw in me.

We'd shared an incredibly passionate six weeks before Klaus told me was returning to Denmark for the holidays. He'd only be gone a fortnight, then he would return at the start of January 1991. On 22 December we said a tearful goodbye, and on the twenty-third I received a short letter:

'CJ, I love you very much and I wish I'd met you a month earlier so I would never have left Germany but I'm going to Japan for five years. Goodbye.'

Suffice to say, the season of goodwill was a little lost on me that year. I hardened my heart to never permit that depth of emotion again.

It's no excuse for the way I behaved towards Arthur, and especially Andrew, but that was how I felt. It was a certainty that they'd both leave me, so if I prematurely drove them away it wouldn't pain me as much. As a plan it was ludicrous and cruel. Neither deserved what I did to them, and the fact that Andrew patiently put up with it and understood is mind-boggling.

Eventually, I quietened down and was able to trust him, but I'm afraid to say it took nearly a decade. When someone is prepared to go through such hell from a vindictive and pathetic creature like me, you know it can only be true love.

Coincidentally, it was during each of our stays in Brighton that my life took certain turns, both leading to a common destination. It was 31 December 1999, and as the rest of the country was getting ready to celebrate the new millennium, I was getting ready for bed.

I climbed in at ten and, earplugs in place, was sound asleep by half past. Andrew was out working on a *Big Breakfast* special, so I saw no point staying up if I couldn't be with the love of my life.

Occasions such as birthdays, holidays and new years have never meant anything to me, so we preferred him to earn ludicrous amounts of overtime instead. But it did get me thinking, in the days straight after, about what I wanted to do with my life.

A new era was dawning but, if anything, I was going backwards. I was a layabout grouch, lacking a job or a purpose. Andrew, as ever, was supremely calm and waited for me to find my own path, rather than pressing me to find any employment at all to help with the mounting debts.

I was aware of the urgency, but dared not bring myself to accept anything that risked exacerbating my aimless depression. I half-heartedly went for a brace of interviews at top hotels on the seafront, but although both invited me back for a follow-up, my lack of enthusiasm must have been glaring. One manager asked where I saw myself in a year's time and I responded by saying I expected to have her job. If I'd meant to be witty, I failed, but if my intention was to be bewilderingly off-putting, I was spectacularly successful.

I toyed with the notion of joining an amateur dramatic society to reawaken my dormant aspirations, but tried to convince myself I didn't want to be involved with the amateur circuit when my dreams were much loftier. The candid truth is that I was scared my abilities had waned after so many years, and didn't want to show myself up. I couldn't bear the thought of going for a role in an amateur production and falling flat on my face.

Sheer cowardice kept me from even trying, despite my attempts to believe in a nobler destiny. It's all very well to have an achievable dream, but I lacked the courage to even take that opening step. I worry now that my acting career has suffered without the skills and knowledge I might have picked up.

In early February 2000, I had a minor revelation that perked me up immensely. I'd always had a better than average general knowledge and a good memory, so why not apply for a television quiz show or two? I'd get the chance to win a bit of cash or glory but, if all else failed, I'd get to see myself on the small screen. At the very least, it might provide a slight distraction. After all, it wasn't as if it was going to lead to any sort of career, was it?

7

LET'S GET QUIZZICAL

I applied for a batch of shows simultaneously. As it was my first time out, I considered my chances to be fairly good. Once you've been on two or more programmes, the others aren't interested as the desire is for fresh faces. Every show could, if it wanted, fill its places many times over for each episode in perpetuity. However, because they're so obsessed with diversity, their options are severely restricted.

I've covered this extensively in *How to Win TV Quiz Shows* but it bears repeating: it isn't stereotyping, merely a basic, undeniable fact to say that the vast majority of quizzers, of all abilities, are white, straight, overweight and male.

It's a struggle for any television quiz (I'm making a clear distinction here from game shows, which are rather different) to fill any other quota. If you ever attend a top-level national or international quizzing event, I'd say the men outnumber the women about eight to one. I've played in a few quiz leagues and the disparity was even more pronounced there.

Mastermind is a curious example. It receives countless applications for every series but suffers the same problem that most are from this narrow demographic. Therefore, the producers are reduced to inviting previous contestants back time and time again simply because they provide something different to this tedious norm. Here's a rare occasion where multiple appearances are possible not just on the same channel but on the very same show!

For the overworked researchers on these programmes, it's an immense headache. Positive discrimination, while undesirable, is unavoidable, otherwise the contestants would be downright unrepresentative of the wider population. In addition, television is about entertainment, so quirky, colourful people will invariably have more of a chance than dull, grey robots.

I'm fully aware that various shows have unrealistically large allocations of gay people and ethnic minorities, meaning that the forms received from the bulk of applicants are chucked straight in the bin. It's hardly equitable, but this is a world in which the small screen is all-powerful. Ninety-nine per cent of contestants are instantly forgettable, and they're just the ones fortunate enough to get to play; they represent a tiny sliver of those who wanted to.

The problem is that, when making the applications, people don't recognise this. They use a random scattergun approach in the hope one stray bullet might find its mark. They fail to consider if the show is right for them or, far more importantly, if they're right for the show.

For example, you have a choice between *Supermarket Sweep* and *Who Wants to Be a Millionaire?* You're intimately acquainted with the pricing systems of every major shop in the western world but are flummoxed when asked to name the capital city of France. However, you apply for the one that potentially offers far more monetary reward.

I really can't recommend this approach. With so many stages to get through before even appearing on screen, careful planning is essential. Selection, application, audition, preparation and game-play must all be considered and handled appropriately. It boils down to one succinct piece of advice I offer repeatedly: 'Be realistic!'

I sensed an opportunity, so I made my choices deliberately. It would be my introduction to these production companies and, critically, their introduction to me. I was slim, not unattractive and only thirty years old, so I expected plenty of attention. I surveyed the application forms that seemed to be standard across the board. I made up my funny story, ensured they knew I was gay (whether orientation was specifically enquired about or not), and strove to be witty and self-deprecating. I took my time and tried to make CJ as enticing as possible, while retaining a serious air.

I've seen countless forms destroyed without having been read, especially when it's clear that the applicant has tried to be unnecessarily outrageous to get noticed. Multi-coloured ink, stupid photographs and even piles of glitter have fallen from envelopes, usually straight into the wastepaper basket. Applicants aren't in short supply but the patience of researchers is limited; they have plenty of other people who won't waste their time with silly gimmicks.

I popped my suitably sober letters in the post, slumped back onto the sofa and waited. Only two days later, I had a phone call asking to see me for a show called *Pass the Buck*. I'd watched the first series, hosted by Fred Dineage, which had only recently ended. I'd taken to the format, as all the players had multiple chances to graduate to the prize final. They were even invited back for the next show to try again, which I considered a friendly twist. Only later did I deduce this was simply to avoid getting a new busload of contestants in for each episode, reducing logistics and, therefore, costs. Still, in my innocence at the time, I was glad of the programme's generosity in offering the opportunity for another bash.

I grew increasingly anxious as the day dawned. If I came over as rather arrogant at the audition, nothing could have been further from my intentions. The room groaned with prospective contestants and groups of four were summoned to the front to answer questions on the buzzer. To my horror, this was to be done in front of everyone else, adding to the mounting pressure. I'd unwittingly assumed auditions would be private, or with very limited numbers, but had failed to grasp the time and expense restraints companies were working under. I stood at the front with my three counterparts, worried they might all be better than me, or luckier, and I might not get a word in edgeways.

The human brain is an unfathomably complex machine. Nearly every person has the capacity to remember anything he or she wishes, which would potentially negate the insatiable demand for quizzes. What defines and separates the best quiz players isn't necessarily knowledge; it's speed of recall and anticipation. If I know an answer, I can usually bring it to mind and vocalise it with no discernible delay. Other people may be correct too, but a second or two behind me, by which time it's far too late.

Anticipating an entire question before its completion is an often awe-inspiring talent. I always get a little frisson of satisfaction when I'm able to answer after only three or four words, and a gasp goes up around the audience. Top quizzers have heard so many questions, phrases and word combinations before that they can usually make educated, alarmingly accurate deductions about what directions they are taking. They will have given the correct answer long before the question master finishes speaking. Most people possessing this ability and knowledge prefer to play on the buzzer, given the chance, as it exponentially increases their likelihood of winning. With no shadow of a doubt, I know I do!

Three questions were reeled off in quick succession. They had to be quick, as I buzzed in early and correctly for each one. A faint ripple of applause from the audience lifted my spirits, but the researcher instantly dashed my hopes. They'd seen enough, thank you, so would I please not answer again?

I was stunned and feared I'd blown it by committing that most terrible of sins, being too good. There again, I didn't know the next answer so perhaps it was fortuitous. It at least allowed me to retain my air of mystery!

It also bluntly taught me a lesson I'd take advantage of in the near future: television quizzing is not just about being correct. If it were, the entire genre would be mind-numbingly tedious and unworthy of airtime. As it happened, I needn't have been concerned. They must have liked me, as the next week I was at Granada studios in Manchester to record my first ever quiz programme.

It soon transpired I'd made several significant errors before the cameras started to roll. I now feel qualified to offer advice on how to prepare for such experiences, but back then I suffered accordingly. There are extensive restrictions about what can be worn on screen: no logos, no thin stripes, no tiny dots, no clashing colours and so on, but I was perfectly safe with a stylish, vibrant green shirt.

However, it was quite thin and I'd failed to take into account the obligatory name badge. This was pinned into my rather expensive shirt and, four hours later, when it was removed, two large holes had been ripped in the material as a memento of my day out. The wardrobe staff are always professional, but if you choose to take along something valuable and delicate, the responsibility for damage is firmly yours. The other unforeseen problem was that I was absolutely freezing throughout the entire day. As contestants, we were in the building for about seven hours, even though recording would take no more than an hour and a half. We changed clothes shortly after arriving, so a flimsy, short-sleeved shirt was unlikely to keep me insulated during February in the north of England.

Nor is it ever as warm as you might hope in a studio, even with the lighting up above. These tend to be quite a distance from the floor anyway, and some presenters like the air conditioning turned up full blast. I've seen many floor crews shuffling round in fleeces just to accommodate the host. I was shaking enough due to my nerves, but the shivering must have been a nightmare for the long-suffering camera operators.

I also neglected to ask (but then why would I?) whether

the rules were identical to series one. Once in the studio, I was dismayed to learn that they weren't and the changes would come to affect me badly. Previously, the winner would automatically qualify to appear on the next show, irrespective of how much or little he or she won. The good players could often clean up throughout the week so this rule was discarded. Under the new system, I reached the final but won nothing and was immediately dispatched empty-handed with no opportunity to try again. It's impossible to anticipate every eventuality but these were fairly important points.

Even the host had changed, with Eamonn Holmes taking over. I have to confess that, although I liked Fred, I admired Eamonn's proficiency and infectious joy. He was clearly having fun, and that always helps put us poor saps at ease as we wait nervously beneath the spotlights' glare.

So that was the full extent of my inglorious introduction to TV quiz life. My next audition was for a seminal production, *Fifteen to One*. Many supreme quizzers consider this, in its original incarnation, to be the pinnacle of general knowledge contests. We were to be seen at the town hall in Wandsworth, where over a hundred people had to be whittled down to the lucky handful. I was called up in the second group of fifteen, and we were positioned in the familiar semicircle. I stood in the penultimate place and we were asked questions which would move along the line until answered correctly. Little did I know that my appearance would be guaranteed within one minute.

The opening contestant was asked, 'What is a surveyor's measuring instrument called?' He passed, as did the second player and, amazingly, the next twelve. The rather exasperated researcher turned to me and I offered, 'Theodolite.' I've never seen a facial expression that so clearly registered relief, and I was instantly offered a place. A single word had granted me access to the country's premier quiz show. Who said auditions were tough?

A lady ushered me to the side and, expecting to be given filming schedules, I was a little taken aback by her request. She asked if I'd mind being a standby for a short while. I'd receive a small fee but my meals, accommodation and costs would also be covered. I had no objection to a short holiday, especially at someone else's expense, as it would provide a chance to collect further information on the way the studio worked. This could only help once my turn came around.

I was lodged in a beautiful room at a stunning new hotel down the road from the studio. The office told me that I may, within reason, order whatever I wanted on the company's account. I was the very model of self-restraint. I think my only requested extra was the movie *Star Wars: Episode 1 – The Phantom Menace*. It was horrendous...

Three episodes were scheduled each day, and I wanted to experience as much as I could while the opportunity was available. I watched recording from the studio, the green room and even the wardrobe department. Milling around and chatting to contestants let me in on a range of different perspectives. I expected all those taking part to be confident but the pervading emotion was sheer terror. I wondered why they'd applied if this reaction was inevitable, but knew I'd be no different as my fateful hour approached.

After five shows, the good news was delivered. I'd be taking part in the next game, which was to be the last of my second day. One contestant had been caught in traffic and was running too late to make it, so I was wafted through to makeup and hurriedly prepared.

It was then I caught sight of an awe-inspiring face: Daphne Fowler was talking quietly to some of the other players, and it was evident she was to be on my show. My heart fell, as she was a previous champion and undeniably brilliant quizzer who claimed the mantle of clear favourite. I nonetheless felt elated to have the honour of competing against her, to witness her consummate skill first hand. I never care what someone excels at, whether it's music, quizzing, sport or bricklaying. I will gaze upon it with wonder and appreciation if prowess and grace are exquisitely demonstrated.

A researcher announced our ten minutes' call and set up to deliver our final briefing. At that moment, an embarrassed runner materialised and whispered for me to join him outside. He was hugely apologetic, but the missing player had shown up and was already getting ready. He had to take precedence, but if I'd bear with them they'd guarantee me a place on the very next show. I pretended to be crestfallen, while hiding my glee at avoiding Daphne. As recompense, I made a mental note to take every available extra at the hotel that night. However, he instantly scuppered that plan with the bombshell that I'd have to check out and join everyone else in the approved contestant accommodation.

This was less than auspicious news. We were booked en masse into a truly abysmal hotel near the studio, not a patch on what I'd been accustomed to from the preceding nights. Dingy rooms, dirty conditions and paper-thin walls didn't augur well for the upcoming day. I've always been an incredibly light sleeper and even the tiniest sound will wake me up. One of the greatest frustrations of my life has been other people's noise when I'm trying to fall asleep. Andrew has the enviable facility to sleep contentedly while nuclear devices detonate around him. It takes me an hour or so to drift away, and a butterfly flapping its wings in the Amazon will jolt me promptly awake.

We got to the studio. The parade of briefing, wardrobe and makeup arrived on set with remarkable speed. Amongst my competitors were a previous winner and two successful players from *Who Wants to Be a Millionaire?*, so my hopes weren't high. At random, I was given position four and we waited, on edge, for William G. Stewart to appear. He strode out, very businesslike but with a friendly efficiency, and went through a number of well-rehearsed platitudes.

Then it was straight into game-play. I relaxed after getting my first question correct, and in the second round I was the recipient of an enormous chunk of good fortune. Nominations had started and very soon landed on me. Bill Stewart asked for the name of Charles Lindbergh's famous plane; having watched *The Simpsons* episode in which it features prominently the night before, I confidently answered, 'I believe that's *The Spirit of St Louis*.'

I then chose someone else to answer and she got her question wrong; I chose again with the same result. Whether a testament to my nebulous gift of picking players who were nervous or just not very good, this sequence continued incredibly for eleven questions until a correct answer was finally provided. I think in everyone else's mind this gave the impression I'd spoken a lot and been getting all and sundry correct, so there was little point in picking me. By being avoided for the rest of the round, I astonishingly found myself in the final, standing between and against two ladies.

I had not a clue about the opening trio of questions shared by those either side of me. However, I buzzed in correctly at the fourth, fifth and sixth times of asking, and was presented with the option of another question or nominating. I didn't hesitate to select the latter, and over the next ten cards in Bill's hand I disposed of the ladies.

I burst out laughing in utter shock. I didn't make it onto the finals board but I was a *Fifteen to One* winner – an achievement beyond my ambitions and, if I'm honest, my abilities. I was just monstrously lucky.

After only the shortest delay, I was invited to audition for *The Weakest Link*. It may seem incredible to say this, but I really took a while to take up the offer. It was a wildly popular show, but I disliked the format where the best players could be discarded; it was hardly a game of knowledge. On the other hand, I'd already been on two shows, so this might be my last chance. I grasped the nettle and resolved to organise myself fully.

Appreciating how the television world functions is an essential skill set if you harbour even the faintest aspiration of connecting with it. I occupied only the furthest periphery but wanted to use every scrap of understanding to gain the tiniest edge. I identified the sort of contestant the show usually welcomed and rehearsed my audition technique on that model. This may sound like overkill, and perhaps it was, but I'll simply say this: look at the results!

At the audition, I deliberately got my first pair of questions wrong, launching into exaggerated displays of disappointment.

I gave the impression my third answer was a blind guess, and laughed along with everyone else at my outrageous luck.

At the end of March, I was preparing to travel from Brighton to Wandsworth for filming but was mortified to find we were booked into the same lousy hotel as on *Fifteen to One*. After the crew had deposited us all there for the night, I scuttled over the river into Chelsea and found somewhere a little more to my taste. If I was refreshed and ready for battle, I thought, I'd increase my winning chances and my prize would more than compensate for the outlay. Well, that naïve optimism didn't quite work out.

With polite but stressed efficiency, the next morning we were herded into the green room. As the contestant who started the show was selected in alphabetical order, I asked the names of those present to see if anyone was ahead of me. That little competition was already sewn up, as one young man was called Aaron.

Once the game had started, I lasted a grand total of three rounds. I was the strongest link overall but that's never any guarantee of success, so I got unceremoniously dumped out. My big plus lay in comprehending TV land's machinations. If this was to be my last gasp, I'd make sure it echoed long and loud.

I was led to a room for my post-game interview and, to the undisguised glee of the researcher, let rip. I'd carefully written and edited what I'd say if I had to take the walk of shame, and had no intention of holding back:

'It's pretty obvious they're all idiots, they're all off my holiday list and I hope they never win another penny. I hope them, their loved ones and all their pets die horribly in freak yachting accidents.'

It was anything but spontaneous, but I wanted to be a professional actor so I'd learned my lines (the last bit is actually from *Blackadder*) and knew how to deliver them. The crew tried to recover themselves and look taken aback, but I knew full well they were licking their lips with delight. If nothing else, this would make damn good television!

I realised there was little point in being demure or polite. It was all painstakingly rehearsed in front of a mirror to achieve the main aim of making it sound real, angry and memorable. I believe I succeeded, as demonstrated by the media response the day after the episode was shown. I was criticised, abused and insulted, and I'll give you two guesses as to precisely how much I cared.

The producers of *The Weakest Link* predictably loved the furore and invited me back for a primetime *Bad Losers' Special*. This was to be filmed in the hallowed halls of Television Centre in Shepherd's Bush, so I immediately said yes. It would stand as a nice coda to my quizzing forays, and might serve as a nice finger gesture to those who voted me off the daytime version.

That was how I felt at the time, but here and now I must offer my gratitude to those other players. If they hadn't despatched me, a whole sequence of unlikely events wouldn't have taken place (such as the opportunity to write this book). I'm not daft enough to believe in fate, or to claim that everything happens for a reason, but this wild tangent led to a lot of wonderful things for me. Wherever my fellow contestants from that day in Wandsworth are now, I honestly say thank you.

It became apparent very quickly that most of the others on the *Bad Losers' Special* deserved to have been voted off, as they were just terrible. I was never left with any money to bank and, although the two other best players and myself succeeded to the last three rounds, not a pound more was added to the prize fund. I won £1,650, which, at the time, was the lowest total ever given away on *The Weakest Link* and remains the most miserly ever for a primetime edition. Then again, I'd emerged as victor and had a bit of cash to my name. My television quizzing career had ended with a fifty per cent success rate and some indelible memories.

Except, of course, it hadn't ended! If it had, you wouldn't be reading this book now, would you?

Out of the blue, production companies started calling me up, inviting me to be a contestant on their shows. This was unheard of, and I asked one young man why I'd been targeted. He seemed reluctant to tell me but, after dithering to find the right words, he commented, 'We enjoy your forthrightness of opinion.'

He meant I had a big gob and wasn't afraid to use it. Well, fair enough, he was right. As it meant all-expenses-paid trips to various cities, national exposure and chances to win money and prizes, I thought I'd make the most of this bizarre little sideline that had opened in front of me. I appeared on, amongst others, *Wipeout, Countdown, 100%, 100% Sex, No Win No Fee, Beat the Nation* and *Wheel of Fortune*.

Especially memorable was *Wheel of Fortune*, as I've never been treated so wonderfully. The show was filmed in Glasgow, so I expected a train ticket and single room in a budget hotel. I was actually flown business class from Gatwick, met by a private car and taken to a five-star hotel where a suite and expenses account were placed at my leisure. I can't imagine these courtesies were extended to everyone who took part, so I was amazed and grateful.

Then again, perhaps it spoiled me for other productions that didn't offer the same. I'd had a brief taste of the highlife and took umbrage if someone else's budget couldn't stretch to similar lengths.

During the show itself, I won three prizes but not the final, which went unclaimed. The clue was a two-word film title of six and four letters, with only a solitary E revealed. I can't see many people guessing *Coyote Ugly* from that! Nevertheless, it was a profitable haul from my most enjoyable trip to date.

*　　*　　*

During this period, Andrew and I had moved back to London and were living on Finborough Road in Earl's Court, which backs onto Brompton Cemetery. It was a basement flat, but it never felt like home to me. Something pretended to be a small garden at the back, but it was a nightmarish tangle of thick brambles, thorns and nettles. With a prolonged burst of energy, over two days I completely cleared this jungle away, shedding copious amounts of blood in the process.

We sold the place after less than a year and made a direct beeline back to the centre of Brighton. Unfortunately for the young girl about to move in, two days before we were due to leave, a moron crashed a stolen BMW into our outside railings, leaving the front of the car overhanging our front door. He ran off, leaving the engine still running, dangling precariously in its rather scary position.

Shortly prior to moving into Finborough Road, I'd noticed

a small lump on the roof of my mouth. I pressed it with my tongue but, as I felt no tenderness or pain, I dismissed it as a small blister or ulcer. As always happens, the longer you live with something, the easier it becomes to disregard, and it took six months for me to raise even the remotest concern.

The ulcer hadn't disappeared and seemed, from what I could tell by feeling around it, to have slightly increased in volume. I went to the bathroom mirror, positioned the light correctly, opened my mouth and was horrified by what I saw. A golf ball-sized growth protruded from the upper palate, a ghastly pale grey in colour with faint blue lines like veins crossing over it. I was so accustomed to its presence I was unaware of how big it had become, but it was actually now pressing down on my tongue and restricting movement.

I called Andrew at work and we met up at Charing Cross Hospital shortly afterwards. I spoke to the receptionist and showed her the growth. Within ten minutes I was sitting on a bed, curtains pulled around, speaking with a doctor. He looked and prodded and told me I'd have to be prepped immediately for an operation.

I've never been one to believe ignorance is bliss and definitely prefer to know everything that's going on, no matter how unsettling. I asked him to make whatever calls he needed, but then to calmly sit down and tell me what I was to expect. He suspected the growth was a cancerous tumour requiring immediate excision. If this could be done quickly, the surrounding area could be examined in case the tumour had spread, but it appeared localised so extra risk was minimal.

However, there was no time to lose. Andrew was assured it was a standard procedure and, as we lived very close by, he was advised to go home. I shouldn't have to stay in overnight so he'd be called when I was ready.

I was wheeled straight into the operating theatre and various nurses crowded around me. One told me she was going to administer anaesthetic but suspiciously kept the syringe hidden behind her back. Knowledge is power and I asked her to please show me. Except in this case, I think I made a teensy mistake. The monster she revealed was less a hypodermic syringe than an industrial jackhammer. It made the pitiful thing forced into my buttocks for the syphilis treatment look like a kid's toy.

It was only a local anaesthetic as I was to remain conscious throughout, so she injected four shots into various places inside my mouth. I don't mind needles at all, but that superfine thread being pressed repeatedly and deeply into my gums was really quite nasty. Even now, my jaw tightens up just at the thought of it.

Difficult as it was from my supine position, I tried to take note of what was going on about me. I did notice one machine that bore a striking resemblance to a coffee maker, swirling with red liquid. It took a moment to realise this was the blood being sucked out of my mouth, as the doctor was sawing into the bone to make a hole and remove the entire tumour. I'm no fan of horror films as I don't care for gore fests designed merely to frighten, but I'm in no way squeamish. In spite of this, if you're going to start hacking away at bits of me, at least have the common courtesy to put me to sleep!

The operation lasted about two hours, and I was mercifully allowed to sit up. Without notice, a glass tube full of clear liquid was held up in front of my startled eyes, and I beheld what had been removed from my mouth. It looked horrible and sickly, which of course is exactly what it was. But it held a morbid fascination, as it looked like the skin hanging off zombies in every apocalypse movie you've ever seen.

I was barely able to speak due to the lingering numbness, but expressed my profound thanks as best I could. I looked at the inside of my mouth with a hand mirror, and a hole about three centimetres across was visible in the upper left side. The doctor told me I should be careful for the time being, but the skin shouldn't take too long to start growing over, allowing a complete seal.

He was right, but it in fact it took five years before the hole vanished for good. This was the most terrifying health scare I'd ever gone through. It was cancer – real cancer – and I'd been incredibly fortunate it had been confined to such a small area. I was even more fortunate to be in Britain, where the incredible staff of our National Health Service had speedily saved my life.

It makes me furious when I hear people – often wealthy people who've never experienced the NHS in person – banging on about abolishing it or paring it back. In December 2012, Prince Charles – not, I understand, a regular user of such public services – openly said that NHS workers should be more compassionate towards their patients. I'm sure they all thanked him for this advice; it must never have occurred to them to adopt this revolutionary approach. Pontificating on an issue without direct experience or the capability to change it seems rather arrogant. If Mr Windsor wanted to help, perhaps he should have volunteered to work as an orderly for a week.

The NHS is an institution that should be sacred and remains, notwithstanding its problems, the gold standard for the whole world. Take a moment to think how improbably lucky you are to have been born in a country with comprehensive, free healthcare. Then consider all the billions of human beings who could never even dream of such a thing. It's unusual even in Western Europe, and we take it for granted every single day.

Yes, there are problems with procedures, people and funding. People die unnecessarily, waiting times increase and negligence persists. When I'd left London and was living in Brighton, I fell very ill and spent three days in bed with the curtains closed. I reluctantly called the local doctor, who came round with an attitude that made it very clear I was inconveniencing him. He stood at the opposite side of the large bed and insisted I pull myself over to him, looked at me for a few seconds and scolded me for having wasted his time for nothing more than a cold. He left, slamming the door behind him.

The next morning, I felt much weaker and literally crawled to the bathroom. I looked into the mirror and saw a gaunt, bright-yellow face returning my gaze. The local hospital was only half a mile away, albeit up a rather steep hill, and yet it took me over an hour to drag myself there. The staff immediately bundled me into a private room and I was diagnosed with hepatitis.

I was only released after a week and returned home to find a very stern message on my answering machine from the health centre, demanding my details so that the callout doctor could submit his invoice. I went straight round and very loudly told them what had happened, and how I'd be reporting the doctor for his behaviour and incompetence. I received an apology shortly afterwards but still made my complaint.

This awful incident doesn't change the immutable fact that we, in Britain, are exceptionally well off to have this literal lifeline at our disposal. Without those doctors on that day, I may very well have died, and because of that I will always support the NHS. As a small token of my gratitude, I made a donation to the hospital's HIV clinic where I'd had some blood tests in the past. It didn't amount to much, but it was all I could spare and every little helps with such causes.

When I've allowed my liberal tendencies free rein in the past, I've argued about the necessity of the nuclear deterrent. I agree we need one, but is the latest missile that might kill ninety-one per cent of a hostile force rather than ninety per cent really worth upgrading to? I'm not desperate to have the latest model of anything (and I definitely haven't put my name down for the newest iPhone), and one weapon of total annihilation seems pretty much on a par with any other. Couldn't we please pump those billions, even for just one year, into our health service? I'd suggest that's a much more effective way of saving lives than threatening to launch a big bomb.

* * *

While I was obstinately ignoring the cancer threat in my mouth, I helped out with various television pilots and rehearsals. One particularly sticks in my mind, as it was too appalling to behold. Myself and four others were asked to consult on a suggested format tentatively entitled *The House*. This centred round the concept of inviting several couples to stay in a large house and the last one in place would win the property. Fair enough, I thought, and I waited to learn about the series of challenges and quizzes they would have to overcome.

It was to be nothing of the sort. It resembled *Big Brother* but was considerably more malicious. Each couple was encouraged to be as nasty and repulsive as possible, to force the others to leave in disgust or tears. The viewing audience was to be presented with the ultimate in car-crash television. An executive from the production company asked each of the five consultants in turn what we thought. I was last in line, and after listening to the mindless yes-men enthusing, I let him have it:

'It's an obscene concept and whoever conceived it shouldn't have been conceived themselves. I beg you, for the sake of your company and reputation, not to go ahead with such a voyeuristic abomination. Bury the entire thing in a very deep coffin and deny all knowledge of it with the vehemence of a thousand fiery suns.'

He clearly wasn't expecting such an onslaught, but I suspect I was the only person to tell him what he needed to hear. Unless he threw himself in the deep coffin too, he must have taken it to heart, as this hideous idea has never seen the light of day.

There was no way of knowing it but one such contact would ultimately transform my life. I was walking in central Brighton one Tuesday evening when my mobile rang. It was a woman from 12 Yard Productions, a company I hazily recalled from rehearsals I'd helped out with some months before. She was in a panic as they were due to film an episode of the show *Without Prejudice?* the next day, but one of their panellists had abruptly dropped out. She asked if I could possibly come up the next morning and take her place. I checked my diary and, as it was empty for the foreseeable decades, I happily agreed. She explained it would be all expenses paid, with a car laid on to take me to and from the studio, and I'd even receive a fee. My agreement suddenly got a lot happier!

The programme was fine. I produced a tasty selection of the soundbites I knew broadcasters drooled over. They especially enjoyed, 'I try not to like people. It makes the holidays much more affordable.' It was nice to meet the host, Liza Tarbuck, as Andrew had worked with her several times on *The Big Breakfast* and she'd repeatedly praised his work.

Following this, as 2002 closed, I'd exhausted the rota of available programmes, so I accepted that my dalliances with the small screen had come to an end. They'd lasted three years and had often been as exciting as they were utterly unpredictable.

But I did want to use my fee from *Without Prejudice?* for something useful, so I booked some driving lessons. I was aware of the basics but had never progressed beyond them, and at thirty-two years old it was about time I learned. However, as a confirmed city boy – or so I felt – it was doubtful I'd ever really need the skill.

I had to come to terms with normality though, and thought gaining my licence might be something physically tangible I could take from my pseudo-celebrity excursion. I believed that brief part of my life was now over, but, less than four weeks later, I took another call and realised how very wrong I was.

8

EGGHEADS (WELL, WHAT DID YOU EXPECT?)

'm not sure of the exact date, but it was around mid-January 2003. Andrew was driving through Barnes in southwest London with me as passenger. Certain tiny details from specific days can never be erased, and I can picture this scene with searing clarity. We were passing Rosslyn Park rugby ground at 11.30am. I was intently watching the gear changes and pedal movements, figuring that the more I observed and learned here, the less I'd have to shell out for my lessons. I was annoyed to be snapped out of my concentration by my phone ringing but fished it impatiently from an inside jacket pocket. I stabbed at the answer button as Andrew drove on.

It was another young woman from 12 Yard Productions, asking if I'd be free to come into central London the next week. They wanted my help with a read-through for a new quiz show idea in development. I really wasn't that keen to invest a whole day, requiring dreary train and taxi journeys, merely to read for some nebulous new idea.

I expressed my sincerest thanks for considering me, and was about to decline when she piped up, offering another fee. Laziness may be one of my less attractive qualities, but stupidity certainly isn't. I confirmed I'd be ready and willing, wherever and whenever they wanted me. I enquired about the format and she told me it was loosely based on a quiz idea from *The Guardian*, called *The Dream Team*.

I vaguely recalled this was where the newspaper had taken a team of top-level quizzers to various pubs throughout a week to see how many quiz nights they could win. They ended up being successful in six of the seven, so it was branded an interesting social experiment and put to bed.

12 Yard's executives had picked it up and meticulously expanded it for the BBC. Another name, intended to describe the resident quiz experts in a reverential but self-deprecating way, was proposed. This new show was to be called *Eggheads*.

A group of us met at an office block just off Regent Street six days later. There were staff members from 12 Yard and the quizzers, myself very humbly counted amongst them. I was introduced to Chris Hughes and Gavin Fuller, both of whom had won *Mastermind*, Amy Godel, a well-known, successful participant in quiz shows, and another chap I have no recollection of!

(I'd not seen him before and I'm afraid his name is lost to me. So if you're reading this, mystery man, please forgive my forgetfulness.)

We were asked various questions to gauge our abilities,

but there was no way I could possibly compete on an equal footing with my illustrious counterparts, so I emphasised the personality aspect. This was a conscious effort to inject humour and balance the studious approach of everyone else. I gave my fair share of answers, usually picking up the popular-culture themes like identifying Skeletor as the archenemy of He-Man, but stayed steadfastly nonplussed when levels rose to the academic.

I've never been one for playing showbiz games and find the thought of celebrity parties and awards shows off-putting. Unless it's for a charity I support or there's someone I'm really keen to meet, I turn down every one I'm offered. A forced smile makes my face ache after only a few minutes; after an entire evening, it'd resemble a crack in the walls of hell. Therefore, when we were asked for our thoughts after an hour or so, I responded with ill-advised honesty.

The sensible thing would be to push CJ de Mooi as the obvious candidate for the programme, but instead I dismissed myself as not good enough. I recommended Kevin Ashman and Daphne Fowler, both of whom must have been on the company's radar anyway. I insisted it would be impossible to have a supreme quiz team if either of these brilliant players was absent.

I was thanked for my time and informed a taxi would be ordered. I preferred to walk back to Victoria, as I had two hours until my scheduled train. During my stroll through the backstreets of Mayfair, I calculated what my hourly rate was for my day's work and felt altogether satisfied at the figure. My thoughts then turned to another sum and my spirits plunged.

A vast number of format ideas are presented to production companies every year. Of these, let's optimistically say ten per cent reach the stage of a read-through similar to the one I'd just done. Ten per cent of those get to be seen by a broadcaster, with ten per cent receiving funding for a pilot. From then, only – you guessed it – ten per cent are commissioned, and only ten per cent of what's left see more than one or two series. The chances were statistically almost insurmountable, but I took solace in not feeling so bad about ruling myself out of consideration. I heard no more about it.

In the second week of March, Andrew and I were off on holiday to Pangkor Laut in Malaysia. Although it was a beautiful island and very quiet, I felt apprehensive as it meant a week of enforced relaxation, which, ironically, was bound to make me very tense.

I took along a large pile of books and finished four, including *Gulliver's Travels*, during my luxurious imprisonment. Despite my best efforts, I did start to enjoy myself, especially during my personal highpoint when we were ferried, with a picnic basket, to a small desert island some miles off and stayed for the whole day.

I have to say with regret that I wouldn't go back to the country now, due to the aggressively hard-line approach of its government. It's yet one more stunning country with lovely people that's been shamefully ruined by the fervent beliefs of a tiny few at the top.

We returned. All had gone silent on the *Eggheads* front, but I did pick up a message about rehearsal for a new show called *19 Keys*. There was a small fee if I could come in and help with some filmed run-throughs. We'd spent more than planned in Malaysia, so every penny was welcome and I eagerly attended.

I liked the host, Richard Bacon, and the format, but identified two major weaknesses. Firstly, any decent player would just annihilate the field and win every game, so the selection process would have to brutally scrutinise everyone. Secondly, the element of luck played too large a part. Four players took part and three could answer all the questions correctly, with the fourth contributing absolutely nothing. However, at the end, that passenger could buzz in and have some chance of taking the money home. I thought this mightily unfair and explained my reasoning to the staff. They nodded appreciatively and made copious notes; after all, this was why they'd called me in.

I departed, happy with my contributions and watched the show's opening episode a few weeks later. My suggestions had been completely ignored and the game-play was unchanged from the rehearsal format. It lasted one series of twenty shows and sank without trace. As a personal hero of mine, Sheldon Cooper, would say, 'I informed you thusly.'

At the height of summer 2003, I spent most of my lazy days in the gym, in front of the television or on the nudist beach near Brighton Marina. This isn't some seedy pickup joint for gay guys – although quite a bit of that goes on – but a casual, friendly place for couples, families, children and pretty much everyone. I was almost able to relax down there, whenever I could find a reasonably quiet spot, which presented a challenge during the warm weather. The only problem with Brighton is the total absence of sand. The entire beach and seafront are covered with large pebbles, so it's a trial to find comfort. Staggering barefoot (and bare everything else) from the water back to your towel means running a very slippery, treacherous gauntlet.

One afternoon in the middle of June, I went down to the nudist beach with my friend Andy and his girlfriend. Almost straight away it turned cold, so we packed up and left. We ambled over to Kemptown to find somewhere to eat, and I noticed a missed call on my phone from an unknown number. My usual reaction is to ignore such things. If it's important, they'll leave a message or call back; if not, it's probably an unwelcome cold caller.

We had a meal in a pub with a rather gloomy panelled interior, and went our separate ways after our disappointingly abbreviated day. I rarely have my phone's ringer turned on so I hadn't heard a second call but saw a message had been left this time.

I waved off Andy, began to make my way back into the city and switched on my voicemail. It was yet another young woman from 12 Yard – how many did they have? I think her name was Sarah, and the message asked me to call back as soon as I could. I lacked the eagerness to discuss more format ideas while on the move, so I slipped the phone away and didn't retrieve it until I got home half an hour later.

I called the office and asked for the lady in question, before proceeding to one of the most curious, and possibly most important, conversations of my life.

'Hi, it's CJ. You asked me to call back?'

'Oh, hi CJ. Thanks for getting back to us. Listen, we've got great news. *Eggheads* has been commissioned!'

'Oh, that's wonderful. So you'd like me to come in and

help with more read-throughs?' I at once sensed the chance to make a bit of extra money, and wasn't about to be shy.

'No, we've done all that.'

'Ah, so you want my help with rehearsals?'

'No, no, that's all finished too.'

'So you want me to come in and help with a pilot show?'

'No, that's been filmed already.'

By now, I was thoroughly confused and more than a little irritated.

'Uh, okay. So why are you calling me exactly?'

'Well, we start filming in a few weeks, so get revising!'

I was well and truly flabbergasted. I asked her to slowly, methodically explain what she meant. Apparently, while I'd been away, all the intermediary stages had been given the go-ahead and had taken place. Scheduling had been arranged and recording booked for early August.

The panel of five Eggheads had been selected and they wonderfully, inexplicably, wanted me to be one of them. If I expressed willingness, someone else would call later that day to discuss all the necessary details. I was understandably intrigued and honoured, but merely said I'd be happy to talk about it. I'm not sure why I was playing hard to get, but perhaps I relished having someone chasing me for once, rather than the other way around!

I was sitting in the lounge of our flat, facing the main dome of Brighton Pavilion, as the phone dropped from my ear. I couldn't process what had just happened. Even though my immediate instinct was to call Andrew, I couldn't put into words what I wanted to say.

I pressed the two buttons to speed-dial his number but

was redirected to his voicemail. I left an unnecessarily brusque message demanding a return call as soon as humanly possible, and sent a text to the same effect. Directly on putting the phone down, it rang and I snatched it up, expecting to tell Andrew the news. Instead, it was a young man from 12 Yard (not all women there, then) to brief me fully on the new show that I was, for some reason, to play an integral part in.

The series would consist of thirty shows to be transmitted on the BBC. The intention was for them to go out later that year but the date and timeslot were unconfirmed. We covered logistics, recording schedules, studio rules and significantly, salary. I could hardly believe somebody was actually going to pay me for my hobby, and on national television no less!

I was warned about an impending flurry of phone calls, emails and letters over the coming weeks, but my growing excitement had already banished any butterflies I may have been feeling. I was giggling uncontrollably by the time I hung up. I didn't even register the missed calls and texts from Andrew until I'd quietened down.

Very soon he rang back, and we spoke incredulously about the gift horse I was staring at. I recognised I'd got the place on the panel due to my personality, but that was never going to be an adequate substitute for real knowledge. I didn't have long, so I needed to hit the books hard and get learning.

But where on earth was I supposed to start? I determined what I thought were the basics and tried to fix upon those. If you're an aspiring quizzer, there are various things you just have to know. The only safe ground is to be completely au fait with British monarchs, capital cities, flags, US presidents and important dates. These are all inescapable topics that must be learnt backwards. With so little time available to me, I also watched every quiz show I could find to see the sort of stuff that was coming up, and perhaps catch some of the regular questions. Andrew was made to trawl through piles of quiz books, asking me thousands of questions. Personally, I've always found it easier to remember answers by this method than if I physically see them for myself.

I grabbed a few friends and dragged them to pub quizzes in and around Brighton. It's a shame, but I don't do this anymore as quizmasters have become so lazy. They simply download any old rubbish from the internet and allow players to cheat constantly with their mobile phones.

I have to say that neither of these is a problem when I host a quiz! To ensure it's done properly, a single question should take an absolute minimum of fifteen minutes to write. It needs to be thought of, phrased correctly to avoid ambiguity and verified twice from reliable sources. Even with instantaneous information at our fingertips, this is a laborious process. Also, before every one of my quizzes my cautionary spiel is always the same:

'Ladies and gentlemen, in the interests of fairness for everyone, no mobile phones!'

A round of applause usually greets this statement. Clearly, many other people have been as annoyed as I by the lax approach in pub quizzes.

'I don't want to see anyone using a mobile phone for any purpose while a round is active. I don't care if you're making a call, receiving a text, taking a photograph or using the phone to scratch yourself intimately. If I see you, I'll deduct you points and not even tell you. Each of the rounds only lasts ten minutes and if you're unable to cope this long without using your phone, I respectfully offer you these two pieces of advice: find another quiz and get a life!'

Now there's raucous laughter intermingled with a few people fidgeting as they realise I'm deadly serious.

'Now, does everyone understand my rules about mobile phones?'

Cue frantic nodding of heads and grunts of approval.

'Not that I could come close to caring, but does anyone disagree with my rules about mobile phones?'

A resounding roar of 'No!' goes up and I begin.

It's surprising how many try and get away with it. But I will not permit cheating and that's why people like my quizzes. Believe me, when I give an instruction, I mean it earnestly, but some teams have doubted my sincerity to their cost.

At an event I was hosting in Preston, a team was leading by a mile into the last round when one female member took a call. She dismissed me with a laugh and a wave as I made an announcement over the microphone. She was later dismayed to discover I'd deducted her team the precise number of points they were ahead of fourth place, completely relegating them. She launched into a foul-mouthed but ultimately fruitless tirade, loudly complaining to all and sundry. She'd heard what I'd said but elected to ignore it.

I don't say these things to be vicious, but I do insist on a level playing field for everyone so we can all have a good time. If I'm in charge, these are my inviolate rules; if you break them, it's your choice. Any quizmaster who doesn't act so resolutely encourages cheating, is disingenuous to his paying customers and frankly useless at the job.

* * *

I loved this brief period of soaking up information but was acutely aware of the time restrictions I was under. All too soon, the date to travel to London was upon me and I made my way to the city. 12 Yard had offered me hotel accommodation, but I was so nervous that I needed a calming influence around me, so I stayed with my friend Pete in Teddington.

I'd got to know him when living in London previously, around the same time he'd started dating his new boyfriend. Unfortunately, this guy was HIV positive; he transmitted the virus to my friend without informing him of his status, and duly buggered off.

Pete was such a lovely man; we even went to New York for a weekend together while he was ill. He was intelligent, patient and loving, just the sort of person I needed by my side to keep me grounded. Coming back to him each evening would prove invaluable, and prevented me walking out on the show when it had barely begun.

I arrived at Television Centre the next morning, visibly shaking with nerves. A car had been sent for me, and I was whisked to White City, through the imposing security gates and up to the main building.

I stared into the famous doughnut courtyard with the glittering statue of Helios at its centre. I'd seen this image so many times on screen but never thought I'd be here, blinking at it with my own eyes.

A runner greeted me in reception and she introduced me to the other Eggheads as they arrived. I'd already met Chris Hughes, but joining him were the inestimable Daphne and Kevin. Even though I'd had my previous near miss with Daphne, I'd never met her and Kevin was a completely new proposal. I was the youngest Egghead by a considerable margin, and it was an occasionally worry that some from the older generations might be bigoted or right-wing, homophobic or racist. For these three lovely people at least, nothing could have been further from the truth. Indeed, Kevin and Daphne would be guests when Andrew and I had our civil partnership ceremony in 2008.

Of course, these concerns aren't limited to older people, although as a populace we are thankfully growing more liberal and tolerant. Due to the constant use of social media and internet broadcasts, each new generation tends to be more open and accepting than the preceding one. Individuals and factions persist, but as the average membership age of political parties such as the Conservatives and UKIP moves above sixty, the pervading trend is towards acceptance.

I've been on one Gay Pride march and to one Pride festival in my life, and neither was a particularly enticing experience. But whatever they were for me is irrelevant, as I can fully understand and support the reasons they exist. In Britain we are still some way off equality for everyone, but we're getting closer. As I work in television and theatre, I'm cocooned in environments where people's differences aren't discriminated against – or, for that matter, celebrated. We just recognise we're all the same underneath and get on with our jobs. I doubt it'll happen in my lifetime, but I'd love to see everyone in this country adopt that simple approach.

*   *   *

The familiar routine of wardrobe and makeup followed, but the briefings were far more frequent and intense. I was now on the other side, no longer a contestant but part of the programme. An industry insider!

None of the Eggheads was allowed anywhere, not even to the toilet, without a chaperone. Perpetual surveillance was our personal bondage. The dearly lamented Television Centre was an infamous maze, notoriously easy to get lost in. It would take me four series to confidently navigate my way around, by which point I was the one guiding the ever-changing crew of 12 Yard runners around the place. Some of the lower levels were just endless rings; you might find yourself literally walking round in circles. You wonder where all those beloved presenters and actors of yesteryear are now? The poor sods are still wandering around in the basements of Shepherd's Bush somewhere, unable to get out...

The host was to be Dermot Murnaghan, but I was unsure how to react to this. He'd only presented one previous light entertainment show, the final series of *Treasure Hunt*. I've no idea if it was intended to be the last, but it must have been an enormous task to emulate the team of Anneka Rice and Kenneth Kendall. Dermot did what he could, with Suzi Perry assisting on the ground, but the chemistry and mischievous fun seemed to have been lost.

Treasure Hunt ended immediately prior to *Eggheads*, so I was a little wary. Then again, he was an experienced television presenter and newsreader, whereas we were untested newbies. I imagine he was just as wary of us, with far more justification.

Eggheads' first day would comprise two shows. The normal complement would be four, but in later series this often increased to five. Studio time is so expensive that it makes economic sense to pack as much into as short a time-frame as possible.

I certainly felt no pinch of austerity and was treated very well, but they saved every penny they could to keep costs down. The potential reward for this was re-commissioning, which made even the tiniest scrimping effort very worthwhile.

When you're appearing on television, ninety per cent of the time is spent sitting around waiting. We've now got our technique down to a fine art, but for a day when five shows – each lasting less than thirty minutes – are scheduled to be recorded, a full shift of twelve hours is required. In the early days, we were nowhere near as efficient, so we became very accustomed to hanging around.

I maintained the glorious hundred per cent success rate from winning my first head-to-head only until my very next, when I lost. I was exhilarated but tense, and this came over. I tried to relax and give a little of the performance I'd been employed for. I was obviously meant to provide a little comic relief for the show with my relative youth and more pronounced personality as foils against the serious business of quizzing. I somewhat exaggerated this with my dubious taste in shirts.

The problem was, back then it was proving surprisingly

difficult. Indeed, for most of series one, I looked like a bunny caught in headlights. Yet I went back to Pete's after my first proper day's work in over six years with a satisfied smile. Day two would make thoroughly sure it was slapped off my face.

I played four head-to-heads and lost each one. My record was now one win and five losses, and I was reduced to tears. I've only cried twice in the last dozen years, and the second was from joy at the civil partnership. This was anything but joyful. I was a distraught, blubbering mess.

The producer, Jim, tried to console me but I burst out, 'Why the hell have you invited me onto this show? I told you I wasn't good enough and now I've just proved it for the whole country to see!'

He tried to soothe me with platitudes about giving the challengers a chance and how it made for good viewing, but it was hardly what I needed to hear. I thought I'd care more about putting on a good show than getting the silly questions right, but I'd been kidding myself. It would take years to become skilful enough to combine the two successfully, but back then I couldn't manage either.

I morosely climbed into my waiting car and left, in two minds about whether to return for day three. I didn't want to depress myself by repeating this almighty disaster, and the programme itself would risk derision if my presence became a glaring flaw.

Back at the house, Pete patiently listened as I whined on and on, only opening his mouth when I finally shut mine. To him, it was obvious why *Eggheads* wanted me – and if I was honest, I was fully aware of it.

I'd played up to a persona at the read-through, and 12 Yard identified that this would be needed to offset the relentless, brilliant quizzing of Chris, Kevin and Daphne. So I should go along with it, play to my strengths and stop moaning.

The recording would be severely edited too, but the more we gave the cameras the greater the options would be for the final cut. The others were there to give the answers, accompanied by long, tedious explanations. My purpose was to counter that with personality, a sense of fun and the unexpected. These are essential components for any entertainment programme, and I was an important piece of the puzzle.

I smiled at Pete's transparent efforts to cheer me up, but it was barely working. I called Andrew and tried not to sound too upset as he pretty much repeated Pete's speech. I thanked them both for their words of kind comfort and promptly disregarded everything they'd said.

Yes, my persona could be the focal point, but I'd much rather get the questions right as an additional bonus. Without further ado, I began to read a quiz book and didn't put it down until well past midnight. I went to bed, resolute that from now on I'd balance the fun and quizzing aspects far more effectively.

Day three consisted of another four shows, and I predictably played a head-to-head in each. It was only towards the tail end of series two that I had the strange experience of not being selected. Then, as happens now, I was quite upset!

That's why the person on each team who doesn't play is nominated as the speaker, to give the final round answers. I think that overall, percentage-wise, Kevin has been chosen the least and I've been chosen the most. Whether they love me or hate me, the challengers clearly want me to have screen time and this isn't something I'm likely to complain about.

There was a seismic shift in those four rounds. I answered every single question correctly, bringing my strike rate back to fifty-fifty, and returned home in a much brighter mood that evening!

Filming continued on the remainder of the thirty episodes, ending the following Tuesday. We hadn't a clue about what would happen when the programme was aired, but 12 Yard presented us each with wonderful gifts. I got a solid wooden box that turned out to be a gorgeous Fortnum & Mason hamper. It was entirely vegetarian and teetotal, so it had clearly been selected with great care.

I was touched by this attention to detail and the speeches afterwards were all very sweet, although palpably tinged with sadness that this might be our one and only series. We said our goodbyes and then *Eggheads*, as far as any of us knew, was over.

I kept my metaphorical fingers crossed for further work, but even if this was in vain, it had been a thrilling ride for which I was unspeakably grateful. For now, I returned to my life of aimless unemployment, living off my partner, fending off ever-growing debts and frittering the days away.

In a blaze of no publicity whatsoever, *Eggheads* almost apologetically slid onto BBC1 at 12.30pm one cold November afternoon. It received an overwhelming reaction; somewhere a dog barked and a lady in middle England tutted. As the series went on, viewing figures were adequate but nothing special. A few bemused reviews started to appear. I particularly liked *The Guardian*, from whence the whole idea had originated, describing me as 'a future Bond villain'.

(Ironically, I was to apply for this very role in *Skyfall* and *Spectre*, but wasn't invited to audition for either. Had these people not read the liberal press a decade before?)

Conspiracy theories rapidly sprang up – and are echoed even today – about how we must have received the answers on set or in advance, and how our questions were so much easier than those of the challengers. All were complete rubbish, of course. A show like that could never get past the watchdogs or fool the viewers.

We'd kick-started something though. The public was morbidly fascinated by the concept of a professional quizzer.

Then came the truly weird experience of being recognised. I was in the supermarket at the bottom of St James's Street, in Brighton, when an old lady came up to me. These days, if fans say hello in the street, I'll be polite, charming and leave them with a photograph, or autograph, and smiles all round within thirty seconds. Sadly, I totally lacked this skill set back then, and the woman kept me talking for ten minutes. Oh, how sweet you might think, but oh dear me, no...

'Excuse me, are you that young man from *Eggheads*?'

'Yes, I am, and thank you. It's lovely to meet you...' I waited for her to introduce herself, but she was more interested in interrogating me.

'It's DJ, isn't it?' She clearly wasn't *that* much of a fan then.

'CJ, actually. How are you?'

'Oh, I love your show. You all just know so much! Let me tell you about my husband's prostate exam...'

The words 'in graphic detail' don't do the ensuing

conversation justice. Never in human history has a conversation between strangers featured the word 'polyp' with such nauseating frequency. But to her, I wasn't a stranger. She'd welcomed me into her living room every weekday for six weeks. I was a familiar visitor.

Nicholas Parsons told me in 2005 – while we were both at a quiz in Tallinn, Estonia – of an experience he once had on the London Underground. He was sitting minding his own business when he noticed the two elderly women sitting opposite peering at him. He smiled and one woman turned to the other, commenting, 'Oh, it's Nicholas Parsons. Doesn't he look old?'

They in no way meant to be rude, but were just so used to seeing and hearing him in their homes that it never occurred to them that he could see and hear them too. Fortunately, as a kind and generous man who's been in the business long enough to know, he just stayed quiet.

But there's a dangerous flipside to this when one starts to expect the attention. A couple of years later, I was playing Judas (no typecasting there, then) in a Manchester production of *Godspell*. Just before opening night, we all decided to go out to dinner at a lovely Italian restaurant in the city centre. We piled out of the cabs, only to find ourselves face to face with a group of expectant photographers crowded around the front door.

I thought – or, if I'm more honest, naively hoped – that they were for me. As I approached one lifted his camera, only to drop it immediately on deciding I wasn't worth the trouble. Were they really going to stand there for several hours until we left, on the slim chance that I'd be caught somewhat the worse for wear?

We sat down in good spirits and ridiculed them for not having done their homework. A little research would have revealed I was teetotal. We began devising little tricks to demonstrate my sobriety to them as we left. One was to draw out an imaginary tightrope and have me walk along it right in front of their lenses. Oh, how we laughed...

Suddenly, a commotion began outside. Two middle-aged men rushed into the backroom and sat at the next table, just three metres away, accompanied by a huddled black bundle. A hood was discarded, a head shaken and there, jaw-dropping and in the flesh, was Liza Minnelli!

I so desperately wanted to throw myself at her feet, but I get completely tongue-tied with even more minor celebrities than me, so there was no way I could ever approach, in any sense of the word, a superstar.

However, Joel, our cast's lovingly camp little teenager, jumped straight up and said hello to her. I'm not usually jealous, but I was in awe of his chutzpah, and so wish that I'd had the guts to do the same.

We left and a few paparazzi were still lingering around, but by then I didn't care. We'd had a great meal and a friendly evening, but it was dominated by an overwhelming presence so near and yet so unattainable.

I can't imagine how people of that status cope on a daily basis, but it taught me an invaluable lesson. Notoriety and fame are fleeting for all but a few; it doesn't matter who you are, there's always someone more spectacular. Unless, of course, you're Liza Minnelli, in which case there really isn't.

*   *   *

Eggheads may not have been the most exciting programme, but it was a genuinely original idea that had never been seen on television before. That was the hook that caught the imagination and ensured a second series.

About six months later, the call came through to confirm we'd been given the go-ahead, and we all dutifully filed back to the BBC. I knew the five contestants seen on screen always had a standby with them in case of disruption. Each team therefore comprised six people, with one cheering from the sidelines.

This sensible practice continues to this day, but I did wonder if a similar contingency was in place for us. It turned out that it had been, as Amy Godel from the read-through was on permanent call if needed. This was the case for most of the time we filmed in London, but once the number of Eggheads increased, she became literally redundant.

However, on behalf of us all, I'd like to say thank you to Amy. It's a shame we never once got to see her – or her gorgeous red hair – on screen, but we weren't giving up our places without a fight!

I was a little despondent after filming series two. A team of *Mastermind* and *Fifteen to One* champions – essentially another batch of Eggheads – was set to play us mid-series. However, they were, without explanation, suddenly switched to show thirty.

They came on, duly beat us, and hey presto, all the loose ends were tied up and no prize money was left to roll over. Two series were all we were going to get, so it was time to be grateful and say goodbye.

We retained the same timeslot on the same channel.

Episodes thirty-one to sixty flew out across the airwaves. We'd made slight progress in the ratings, but lunchtime programmes aren't noted for their mass appeal so we didn't hope for much.

Then, halfway through the run, the show changed its timeslot. Letters started appearing in the *Radio Times* and daily press, noting how *Eggheads* was one of the most recorded programmes nationwide; 6pm was a little too early for many commuters, but they didn't want to miss it. A phrase that started popping up was 'comfortable viewing'; people were plainly fond of watching while having their dinner. It was a shame there was no more to come – or at least that's what we believed for nine months.

* * *

It was early 2005, and I was staying in south Wales, house-sitting for one of Andrew's work colleagues. The blissful peace and quiet gave a perfect opportunity to work through a large pile of books. However, my quizzing brain had changed my outlook, and I rarely read fiction anymore.

I was driving into Newport one day and my phone started ringing. I pulled into a convenient lay-by, overshadowed by an imposing stone wall of part-Roman origin. I remember the location precisely, as I've run past there regularly ever since we moved to the area in January 2006.

I was astounded to be told *Eggheads* had been commissioned for a further block, albeit of only twenty-five shows. Also, a national Sunday newspaper wanted me to compete in a Celebrity Sudoku Challenge the next day –

despite the fact that I'd never completed one of the puzzles in my life.

I spent the evening and subsequent morning practising furiously, before heading off to the meeting at The Celtic Manor. The reporter gave me the grid and started his watch. I made a big mistake after only a matter of seconds, but spotted it and finished in a touch under three minutes. Out of the twenty-five people to have taken part, I was delighted to finish in sixth place.

This was the first occasion I'd been involved with anything involving the word 'celebrity', and I felt enthralled and deflated at the same time. I've always been a private person, as evidenced by the amount of persuasion it took for me to write these words. The glare of publicity and its inevitable scrutiny frightened me, but one dormant ambition did begin to awaken.

If I was destined for this kind of attention while *Eggheads* lasted, might there be a chance for my acting career after all? That was the overriding impulse that propelled me into series three, which was to see a massive shift in our viewing public.

9

ONWARDS
AND UPWARDS

All of a sudden, it looked as if this silly little TV show might have the appeal to last longer than I'd dared dream of. So I made a radical decision.

Yes, I'd continue with my persona and playing up to the cameras. But I'd better get down to some proper homework too. I set out a carefully detailed plan and conservatively estimated it would take a year to complete. (As it happens, it ended up taking four, but that's beside the point.) I compiled a list of forty classic authors and selected one novel by each to read. I made hundreds of charts and lists for notable historical events and their dates, births and deaths, major sporting achievements and countless other snippets that might prove useful.

As I read quiz books, one theme that arose with regularity was 'firsts and lasts'. We all know who the first man to walk on the moon was, but how about the last? Who won the first Academy Award for Best Actor? These were two fairly innocuous questions, but I bet we've all been to quizzes where one or the other has come up at some point.

I collected similar facts and soon had a wealth of them, so I began incorporating them into my own questions. Over the last decade, I've written questions for several programmes, magazines and mobile apps. These accumulated databases, whether on my computer or in my brain, have grown to be a fabulous resource.

I started taking part in the national and international quiz scenes, which meant a quantum leap in the quality of my opposition. In any arena, Kevin was still the man to beat, but now I was consistently competing against players very close to his class.

A Quizzing Grand Prix Circuit held high-level events each month around central England and, once a year, the British, World and European championships attracted the very best players too. All centred on an exam paper of usually 150 or 240 questions, spanning various categories.

I must have taken part in forty of them, but only twice did I score more than fifty per cent. These were accompanied by several more relaxed team and buzzer quizzes, but it was the papers that were used to determine rankings.

The European championships were always the most interesting and infuriating. As with the Estonian quiz, these were held in different competing countries, the venue rotating annually. The quiz would be set by the home nation. Although England had the strongest, many other teams had impressive quiz pedigrees – especially Belgium and Norway.

This meant the European events were much harder than the standards.

It was the Estonian quiz where I performed best, achieving one of only two notable highpoints throughout these competitions. Over the weekend in Tallinn, there were nine very testing questions on chess history, and I was the only player to get all nine correct. The other success was a side quiz in Altrincham in 2007, where I beat all-comers to become British quiz champion with the specialist subject of *The Simpsons*. I also won the Mensa chess championship in 2001, so I was now the unofficial King of the Geeks!

This reminds me of a hilarious and much repeated interchange between Jeremy Vine and I on *Eggheads* in 2014. I was in the question room and he turned to me, with a gleam in his eye.

'So, CJ, let's call you the King of the Eggheads. Oh, well, no...'

'Come on, Jeremy. You know you wanted to say the Queen, didn't you?'

We burst out laughing at how we'd bounced off and fed lines to each other. Nowhere would that be shown to better effect than in the later *Revenge of the Egghead*.

Two years later, it was Britain's turn to host the European championships. Blackpool was chosen as the venue. I like this town, so I was very happy with the location and arrived to sit the paper in a great mood.

As I struggled through it, I noticed several people getting up to leave, but I had no idea as to why. The questions were hard, as I'd expected, but surely they couldn't be so impenetrable as to stump such an array of brilliant players?

After scoring two out of twenty-five on the Civilisation sheet, I turned my diminishing attention to the Art and Culture section. On question one, I got as far as, 'Which of the lesser known nineteenth-century Ukrainian sculptors...', and then I too walked out. This was the last time I played in a European event. In fact, I entirely withdrew from the Grand Prix shortly afterwards. I'd learned pretty much all I could at this rarefied level, and if I could expect that sort of torture on a frequent basis, I'd rather save myself the entry fee and my ego the bruising.

*   *   *

Before *Eggheads* had been given its brand new home, the timeslot had seemed far more prestigious but considerably more problematic. BBC2 at 6pm had been the slot where programmes invariably went to die, having to compete against the news on BBC1 and ITV, as well as *The Simpsons* on Channel Four. I unswervingly believe that, if *Eggheads* had started in this early evening position, I wouldn't be typing these words right now.

The schedulers knew what they were doing. We had been allowed to gradually build up a solid and appreciative fan base; it loyally moved with us and began to expand. For a while we shared this slot with other shows, but the ratings were undeniable. Any other offerings were mauled horribly, and only *Eggheads* was able to recapture lost figures. Steadily bringing in about two million viewers, and occasionally getting close to the three million mark, we'd only gone and got ourselves a winner!

Our popularity was growing, and we'd become a fixture in the BBC2 schedules. Then, from the outset of 2007, the channel's regular programming for 6pm was dedicated to *Eggheads*. Major events such as Wimbledon, breaking news and the World Snooker Championships may have temporarily usurped us, but we'd return and so would our faithful viewing public.

Slowly but surely, each of us was becoming a celebrity, with all the positive and negative aspects that entails. As the panellist with the most polarising personality, I received considerably more attention. Now, I had no objections to this as I hoped it would benefit my acting aspirations and, far more mundanely, my bank account. *The Telegraph* colourfully dubbed me 'the main hate figure' on the show for my ability to provoke a response. What a great feather in my cap!

According to a BBC executive I was friendly with, I received more hate mail and death threats than anyone else across their channels for two consecutive years! I proudly claimed this as my ASBO and my badge of honour all rolled into one. It was never going to upset me and, frankly, all I cared about was that people were watching. Love or loathe me, it's all the same in my head. The more you complain, the more the broadcasters love it, the more airtime I'm going to get!

When I joined Twitter in 2010, my initial year was one of non-stop vitriolic abuse. Hatred, vile insults, terrible threats of violence and horrific accusations were piled into my timeline constantly. I found it hilarious.

On occasion, some idiots have taken it too far, and I've made reports to the police when direct threats have been made against my friends. It all faded when these people realised it had absolutely no effect on me, and they presumably slithered off to find other trolling targets.

I find this, and them, immeasurably sad. However, I'm more upset by the heart-wrenching tales of people driven to abandoning social media, or even suicide, by constant harassment. Why such inadequate fools feel the need to have a go I've no idea, but if they must, I'd prefer they targeted me rather than someone it would really hurt. We've reached a position in the world today where digital anonymity makes hate a more prevalent and popular topic than love, which I can neither understand nor accept.

We're not the USA. We can barely tolerate winners, never mind celebrate them. In Britain, if you raise your head above the parapet you must be prepared for a barrage of envious potshots. I did, I was and I flourished.

Invitations to celebrity parties and awards ceremonies started to arrive. Except for the first, to the BBC Contributors' Party, I turned every single one of them down. Frankly, drowning in a self-congratulatory deluge of cheap champagne sounds mind-bogglingly dull.

My growing public profile brought with it, as far as I was concerned, a level of responsibility. There are people who milk it for all they can get and refuse to give anything in return, but, as a wet liberal type, that option wasn't open to me.

I began to involve myself with more charities, naturally concentrating on the areas that interested me most: HIV, homelessness, animal welfare and human rights. I was invited to become a patron of The Crescent in St Albans, which offers care and assistance to those living with HIV. I fervently agreed, and have been honoured to join the staff on many occasions both during their in-house efforts and on fundraising events.

I'm also honoured to have worked alongside Amnesty International, *The Big Issue* and the Dog Rescue Federation. It's not until I got up close and personal that I realised how much even the biggest, most famous charities struggle on a day-to-day basis. Most staff members are unpaid volunteers and government funding is a pipedream. They literally depend on the kindness of strangers to keep going.

As you'd expect, I also began to think about what I wanted for myself in the future. All the signs were that *Eggheads* ensured some security, but such things are transient and can change in a heartbeat. I hoped we'd make it to the almost unheard of 250 episodes, but zero guarantees existed.

In the spirit of striking while the iron is hot, I started making tentative enquiries and seeking out opportunities to get into acting. I spent most of my time in central London, cultivating contacts, getting to know the right people and making sure they were all fully aware the theatre was my one true passion.

My main problem was that I'd never performed professionally, and had no training or worthwhile qualifications. I'd have to rely on my slightly recognisable name to get my foot in the door, so I was fortunate that the schmoozing option was open to me.

I spent a fortune doing this, which was only possible as Andrew had reached a new level in his work and was one of the most sought-after people in his industry. He'd designed some notable films and television dramas, and continues to be in high demand.

Of course, I was earning more too, and with our combined

incomes we were finally able – mortgage aside – to clear all our debts. Prior to 2009, spread across various credit cards and loans, we'd amassed a terrifying total of £122,000 between us. We'd constantly lived beyond our means, and owed far more than we could then have realistically hoped to repay.

Banks make it so easy for customers to take money and suggest they top it up with an extension to this card's limit, or that loan's repayment period. They're equally quick to punish those who miss payments, while accepting no responsibility for causing the mess in the first place.

(But at least all those bankers languishing in jail for melting down the world economy and destroying financial institutions can reflect on the error of their avaricious ways. Oh, just a second... not one of those corrupt thieves was jailed. How ironic that their morals remain the only bankrupt aspect of them!)

Over two belt-tightening years we got rid of everything. We cut up the cards, closed the accounts and told the banks to stop offering further services. For so long we'd buried our heads in the sand and tried to ignore the problem. I hear this same story from so many people currently in the same mess we were. Hoping it'll go away doesn't work. Engage with the bank, work out a plan and, most importantly, stick to it! But never lose sight of that glimmer of light at the end of the tunnel. It's very hard work that may take years, but you owe it to yourself to try.

* * *

The worst experience of my new acting career was a pantomime in Clacton-on-Sea. I was looking forward to it immensely as it was my first seaside show; unfortunately, it quickly turned into a catalogue of disasters. I was cast as the Emperor of China in *Aladdin*, but it was immediately clear I wasn't going to get on with the director. He'd also taken the part of the Dame, and it's a truth universally acknowledged that nobody – at least nobody below the level of George Clooney – should ever direct and take a lead role in the same production.

The large theatre was attached to the town hall, and all the people who worked there were delightful. I often crept away at lunch hour to enjoy wonderful chats with them. On the first day, I took the entire company out for dinner at the seafront Pizza Express and was served by the rudest waitress I've ever encountered. I had to politely request she stop swearing and be a little more attentive.

I went back two days later, and she openly accused me of aggressiveness on the previous visit. I promptly left my meal and walked out. For some reason, in Britain we tolerate appalling customer service across the board.

The hotel was very unpleasant too, so I made a report to the council and moved into alternative accommodation at my own expense. Shortly afterwards, perhaps as a result of all these factors combined, I fell horribly unwell and couldn't even drive home for my two days' holiday. Andrew had to make the return journey from Wales to collect me and then repeat it, despite my protests, to take me back. I have never wanted to leave a job more.

Being sick paled against my worsening relationship with the director. As the (albeit low-level) celebrity turn, I was only on stage for about six of the eighty minutes in act one but had a big song and dance number with the Dame in act two to look forward to.

However, on the second day he suggested it was all getting too complicated and might have to be pared back. I interpreted this as he was unable to remember it all due to taking on too much work, but what was I to do?

The big number was cut and the new version lasted a mere seventy-five seconds. It was most strange then, that the day before we opened, he expressed his concerns that act two was now running too short, and so he'd decided to lengthen his scene. I was excited about having the routine back but worried about the lack of rehearsal time. He dismissed this, as he planned to go on solo for ten minutes and do a comedy routine as the Dame. I was livid; if this had been planned all along, it was disrespectful to the entire cast.

I signed up to a few casting websites but purposefully avoided mentioning *Eggheads* when I could help it. My lack of credits was a hindrance, but I stood out for my age, as most around me were fresh out of college. There may have been far fewer roles to choose from, but far fewer people would be trying out for them.

I applied for a short film called *The Renata Road*, auditions for which took place in Preston. The three-and-a-half-hour drive from South Wales was tiresome, but I arrived at the University of Central Lancashire and dutifully did my piece. The director, Ed Greenberg, and I read the script and discussed the characters at some length. He thanked me as I left, with the usual spiel about letting me know within two weeks.

One of the worst things for actors to deal with is lack of information. We generally hear nothing back if we haven't got the role. A simple block email saying, 'Sorry, on this occasion you weren't successful,' can't be that difficult but is apparently beyond the capabilities of most directors.

It's agony for performers as we're often left in limbo, not knowing whether to apply for another part while waiting to hear. Many hold down second and third jobs to finance their careers, and every audition is expensive to prepare for and attend. However, as supply massively outweighs demand, we're treated like cannon fodder. An actor who isn't willing or able to run the gauntlet can always be replaced by hundreds who are.

The stark truth is that over eighty per cent of drama school graduates will never have a professional role, and close to ninety-five per cent will have dropped out of the business by their mid twenties as they need to start earning a salary – any salary – just to survive. Acting is a very harsh mistress, and this kind of treatment wouldn't be tolerated in any other business. We go into it because the love of performing overpowers our hearts and minds and nothing else will ever make us happy.

More than three weeks elapsed and I heard nothing from Ed. But I suddenly received a message from an acquaintance who – through six degrees of separation – had apparently been told what was happening. He congratulated me on winning the lead role in the film, leaving me doubly shocked: I'd only gone forward for the secondary role of a waiter!

Ed called me shortly after to confirm the good news, and in January 2011 I spent a week filming in and around Preston. The final cut lasts a mere nine minutes, but it was the most enjoyable working experience I'd ever had. We were delighted to secure *The Renata Road* a Leicester Square premiere at the Prince Charles cinema, which is a great supporter of new creative talent. This resulted in some fantastic reviews in the national press. Some of the attention must have been due to the novelty of a television quizzer's acting debut, but I think it was primarily down to the skill of Ed and his team. They created a stunning piece of art, and I was humbled to be a part of it. Three years later, I'd come to realise just how important that week working with them had been.

As Andrew and I had reached an oasis of financial stability, we agreed I should invest some money to make inroads into the theatre world. I took producers for lunch at The Ivy, directors for drinks at The Langham and casting directors absolutely everywhere.

I got to know some wonderful people, including Mike Dixon, one of Europe's top musical directors. He was so patient and generous with his time, which he offered for free. I was as yet undecided as to which route within theatre I wanted to take, but he and casting director Anne Vosser coached and offered much-needed encouragement.

I'm a pretty good high baritone singer and musicals fascinate me, so I must also thank musical director Barney Ashworth and Griff Johnson, who helped me immensely with one role I lusted after: that of Teen Angel in the professional tour of *Grease*. This was reserved for celebrities, and Robin Cousins' tenure was coming to an end.

Barney gave me notice of this and I immediately started rehearsing the song 'Beauty School Dropout', which I'd have to sing at the audition. This is a notoriously difficult piece requiring a lot of personality and technique, and a very high and powerful falsetto for the reprise.

After five months of intense practice, I'd perfected the song and I was ready. I think eighteen people were being seen for the role, and I was last on the list. I sang the song perfectly and received an impressed round of applause from the resident director and producer. The casting director whispered to me, as I was making to leave, that I'd been the only one to get it spot on. This put me in very high spirits, and I looked forward to hearing within the promised fortnight.

Four weeks went by and I was back in Lancashire, making another short film with Ed Greenberg. *Epilogue* was a good piece, but perhaps not in the same class as our previous effort. My main memory is of strolling up and down Blackpool seafront in a biting wind, desperately hoping various bits of my anatomy didn't freeze and drop off, for five hours to record a twenty-second scene.

During one of the scenes, mercifully filmed indoors, my phone rang. I was about to go on set to film a sensitive interchange but I took the call, as I could see it was my agent. He'd heard from *Grease* and, despite my being the standout candidate, the producer, who was American, didn't know who I was and had therefore cast Russell Grant as Teen Angel. Russell had recently competed on *Strictly Come Dancing* and was flying high. Although he's a lovely chap and we've since become friends, at the time I was crushed.

I know it's *show business* and this was a purely commercial decision, but I'd put so much into preparing for the role. I'd spent hundreds, maybe thousands, of pounds while racking up countless miles and hours ensuring I'd be the best. Ultimately, I achieved that goal, but it wasn't a consideration for the producer. He understandably wanted the person who would bring in the crowds, and the singing was most definitely reduced to secondary importance.

To his credit, Russell did indeed fill the seats. Barney, the musical director of the tour, says the band regularly had to wait ten minutes after Russell's entrance each night for the cheering and clapping to die down. I wouldn't have got anything like that reaction, so for the producers it was mission accomplished. I'd come agonisingly close to a major role I really wanted, but it might as well have been an ocean away. To use a quizzing analogy, ninety-nine per cent right is still wrong.

After putting my phone down, I turned round and grabbed the first crew hand I saw. It was a young man called Ryan who I'd always fancied, so that worked out nicely. He hugged me as I dropped my head onto his shoulder, disconsolate. The sole positive I took from this whole experience was that, being so devastated, I needed only one take to record *Epilogue*'s very emotional next scene.

Then came a wonderful break and I thought, *Yes, this is it!* I auditioned for the role of Simon in the comedy play *Guilty Pleasures*, which was scheduled to tour nationally for four months. With a celebrity cast including Darren Day, David van Day and Terri Dwyer, it looked like a sure-fire hit. It was set in a ladies' health club that was essentially a brothel where the male staff attended to the clientele's every whim. My character was a bookish nerd who seduces the receptionist, and is a surprise success with the ladies.

I loved the piece and was delighted when the part was offered. I'd always wanted to perform on a national tour and this would travel the entire country, beginning in Bournemouth. We opened to rave reviews and a standing ovation, and the whole company skipped happily back to the hotel for our opening-night party.

In a state of euphoria, I drove home to enjoy two days off before the tour continued in York. I made my excuses and left the party at one in the morning, arriving home at three, still grinning inanely. I'd turned down another play and a low-budget television pilot for the tour, but those missed chances were never going to dampen my spirits. I was so looking forward to the fun of four months on the road.

My mood was about to be very rudely shattered. I woke to find a text waiting for me at 8am:

'We regret to announce the tour of *Guilty Pleasures* has been cancelled with immediate effect.'

There was no explanation, no apology. Fifteen impersonal words left a gaping chasm of joblessness ahead of me. I was stunned and shouted downstairs for Andrew to come up. I showed him the message, but neither of us could think of anything to say.

After gathering my thoughts and waiting until a more respectable hour, I got on the phone. We'd only been paid for the first week of rehearsals, so we were each owed several hundred pounds, but that wasn't of significance for the moment. I spoke to our sound technician who hadn't even been granted the courtesy of a text.

This was apparently the case for the entire backstage crew, as they all turned up at the York theatre as agreed. We were all in the same boat and getting no response from the company, so I contacted Spotlight and Equity, both of which represent actors and technical staff. It transpired that this had happened before with the director and his inner circle, but nobody at Equity had bothered to warn us.

There's a history of treating actors as disposable cannon

fodder, and as we're all so desperate for any work, we'll put up with almost anything. All performers have been in shows that not only didn't pay, but in actuality ending up costing them money to be in!

When cancellations like this happen, for whatever reason – and no doubt some are entirely innocent – the cast are naturally crestfallen but pick themselves up and carry on as, hey, it's just one of those things, isn't it? Not bloody likely in this case!

I sued the company to recover most of my missing wages and so did several others. Although we were successful, there was nothing to stop this director calmly wrapping up his productions and starting another the very same day.

The dream I'd based my acting future on had been ripped away, leaving me in a much worse position than six months previously. I unceremoniously begged to get back one of the jobs I'd rejected, but to no avail. I'd invested so much love and enthusiasm into *Guilty Pleasures*. Now any hopes of an acting career lay shattered around me, and I would suffer financially too.

During rehearsals for the tour that never was, I'd been introduced to a West End director called Drew Baker. I auditioned for him twice, once for a comedy and again for a serious play. On neither occasion did I get the part, but, so he said, this was entirely down to physicality rather than ability.

The comedy, for example, needed an actor who was considerably heavier than me. There's almost nothing I won't do to secure I role I want but gaining weight is one requirement I'd be very concerned about. Then again, just like everyone else, I have my price; if it's met, I'll do whatever's asked. The fee would have to cover a tough personal trainer to get me back down to size afterwards though!

Drew did cast me at his third opportunity as the Major General in *The Pirates of Penzance*. I'm not a huge fan of Gilbert and Sullivan, but this has always been my favourite piece of theirs. I now found myself inhabiting one of their seminal roles, singing perhaps their best-known song. 'I am the very model of a modern Major General,' echoed around my brain for weeks, and, despite the added libretto of two solo and three ensemble songs, this was my centrepiece.

The venue was a shabby but enthusiastically-run small theatre in Romford. To be honest, I didn't enjoy it one bit. The other cast members were quite young, and a few behaved unprofessionally for the whole run. In the penultimate performance, some of the boys decided to mess around and jump on me on stage, despite my wearing nothing but a dressing gown. They twisted my ankle very badly, and it was all I could do not to scream out in pain.

I was still a novice in the theatre and perhaps I should have kept my temper, but I was so angry that I exploded at them after the curtain. My foot was bruised and swollen, forcing me to hobble through the last show, but since it finished I gladly haven't set eyes on them again.

However, during *The Pirates of Penzance*, I got to know the assistant director, Jamie Chapman Dixon, who is now one of my very closest friends. That was enough to allow the whole show to linger fondly in my memory.

Immediately afterwards, the owners of the venue cast me in the lead role of their production of the thriller *Deathtrap*. This is one of my favourite plays, if one can forget the horrendous film version with Michael Caine and Christopher Reeve. The character of Sidney Bruhl is one of those magnificent theatre roles for older actors, ranking alongside Willy Loman in *Death of a Salesman* and Atticus Finch in *To Kill a Mockingbird*. The play has five characters, but Sidney has sixty per cent of all the lines across the two hours.

With memory not presenting a problem for me, I was virtually off book before rehearsals began, but having trouble getting it quite right. There's a very fine line between performing and acting, and it's most noticeable when a theatre actor moves into film or television for the very first time. The instinct is to exaggerate everything so it can be seen from the back of the auditorium, but, with a camera focusing on you, this is unnecessary and looks awful. 'Smaller' and 'realistic' is what's needed, but even with extensive training, it's incredibly complicated to balance precisely.

I was taking the opposite route and this presented some difficulties with Sidney. The figure firmly at the centre of such an intense piece has to move the narrative along convincingly. Yes, of course subtlety is important, but I was used to underplaying everything and concentrating on each nuance. I worked closely with the director, Neil Reynolds, who was superb and supremely patient with me. I think I was scared about playing out to the audience for fear of hamming it up, and so I kept hitting brick walls until Neil gave me the best snippet of advice I've ever heard.

With so many lines, movements and props to juggle, concentration has to burn brightly. The mind must be in a state of constant readiness, anticipating what needs to be said and where. This approach is right for most actors, but patently not for me. So Neil dismissed it and told me, 'Don't think about it and just do it!'

The change was instantaneous and profound. My voice transformed, I relaxed and all at once I became Sidney Bruhl. Yes, I tripped up on some of my lines, but that's what rehearsals are for. I was able to move away from how I'd visualised and heard the character in my head and make him solid and believable.

I now not only understood Sidney; I related to him. Alright, he was a nasty piece of work, but if an actor can't in some way connect with the role, there's no way the performance will be genuine. It doesn't matter how reprehensible the subject, some truth has to be found.

I've always keenly felt my lack of professional training, although I don't necessarily regard it as a weakness. This though was the first invaluable lesson I'd ever been taught by an experienced industry professional, and I lapped it up greedily. Now, I never go into any rehearsals knowing all my lines backwards. I always leave a little wiggle room, in case the way I feel comfortable speaking them isn't what the director wants. Plenty of actors and directors insist on being word-perfect by day one, but in my opinion this is a mistake. Creativity must have room to breathe and explore. I can't work with a director who refuses to listen to alternative ideas and input from actors. Theatre is a collaborative process, not a magical mystery tour of one person's ego.

*   *   *

I continued with *Eggheads* and low-level theatrical fare. The holiday season brought pantomimes, and although I love performing in them – especially as I now insist on being cast as the villain – I've never been a fan of watching them. As a child I only ever saw one and found it tedious and badly performed. It was *Cinderella*, with some local and stupendously unfunny comic I'd never heard of playing Buttons. He was already in his late fifties; even to my young eyes, seeing him letch over the teenage princess was most unsettling.

Panto is a lifeline for many jobbing actors, but the wages they receive are often pitiful. The names get all the money. The bigger the name, the more obscene the paycheck. Five figures a week is quite common for some homegrown stars, and I dread to think what the visiting Hollywood people command. It is incredibly hard work, even though it's looked down on as an art form. You have to act, sing, dance, be funny, be energetic and interact with the audience. I don't know of any other performance skill that requires so many facets, usually while lumbering around in a heavy, sweaty costume. Be as snobby as you like, but an actor who can do panto successfully can do anything!

A few years ago, I was performing at the Lowther Pavilion in Lytham, just down the coast from Blackpool. I love this little place and regularly make a detour to stay overnight when I'm travelling up to Scotland. We'd had a hard time during the run, but I did make a couple of lovely friends: Ian Fox, who played the Dame, and Dave Dugdale, the stage manager. Dave's now a fireman in Inverness, but I still make time to visit him when I can. Two incidents stand out for me from our run of *Jack and the Beanstalk*.

It was 24 December and I was feeling rather unwell. My temper was short, and I had a solo scene on stage, before jumping out of my costume to step inside and operate the giant. As the villain – always remaining in character of course – the children in the audience and even those on stage gave me a wide berth.

I made my entrance and for the only time in my life was rather unprofessional, proceeding to ad lib. I turned and asked all the boys and girls if they were looking forward to Santa bringing them lots of presents that night. They all cheered and squealed with delight of course, but this was to be short lived. I snarled at them and spat out, 'Well, tough. Santa's dead. I killed him and ate him and he was delicious!'

The floodgates opened. The kids cried and the parents looked horrified, shocked at such an evil baddie. This was supposed to be mildly-scary family entertainment, not the cause of permanent emotional scars. The director gave me a huge telling off, which I thoroughly deserved, but I couldn't help noticing his eyes twinkling while he did it.

The penultimate performance of any run is traditionally the one for pranks, and I pulled off the best ever. But it didn't start as my idea.

Halfway through act two, Ian as the Dame was on stage alone, pulling one of the curtains across while singing. Dave was by the side of stage in his usual place, and I was standing next to him waiting to go on.

At every show we stood there making faces and naughty gestures to Ian, trying to put him off. His expression never wavered, but we were determined to get him on our last chance.

I love Dave and we get on so well. I even got him fixed up with the girl who was playing the princess on the show and a month after we wrapped, he and I went to Gibraltar for a break together.

In the interval, he grabbed me and pulled me into the toilets. He turned around and dropped his pants, to my considerable confusion. He said this was how we could bugger up Ian and handed me a thick felt tip. I snatched it off him in glee and bent down. In big letters I wrote, 'I love CJ' on his buttocks, waited a moment for it to dry and pulled his pants back up.

Cackling maniacally, we scurried out in case anyone else came in. We'd have had some interesting explaining to do. We reached the critical point of the show and waited until Ian was midway through his walk, then jumped into action. Dave sprang round and bent over; I ripped down his pants to reveal his bare bum, put my head beside it with a huge smile and stared right at Ian.

He choked on his words, toppled to the ground and burst out laughing. The music track continued but there was zero chance he would regain his composure. He struggled along the floor, desperately tugging at the curtain and gasping for breath.

His eyes were watering when he reached the sanctuary of the wings. He laughed so loudly, and in such a high pitch, that the audience were audibly shocked. The rest of the song was abandoned, and I went straight into my next speech, trying to appear menacing while suppressing fits of giggles. It was a truly wonderful prank with only one minor side effect: apparently it took Dave nearly a month to scrub the writing off his bum. At least, while it was there, he had a constant reminder of me!

10

HAPPY

I asked Andrew if he'd grant me the inestimable honour of entering a civil partnership, becoming my nominal husband. My words were something along the lines of, 'Shall we do this thing then or what?', but that's as romantic and mushy as I get. He agreed, and we set the date for 30 December 2008.

We booked out the Park hotel near Bath and invited twenty friends. Kevin and Daphne were there, as well as Mark Labbett, who is the star of *The Chase* both here and in the US.

It was a beautiful venue and the food was spectacular – although not quite to the exceptional standard it had been at the tasting. I suspect the hotel had brought in a different chef and the level had dropped slightly. Mind you, none of the guests knew or cared, and they were treated to a fantastic night.

The ceremony was pretty brief, but the reception and dinner were somewhat lengthier. We all drifted off to our rooms about 10pm, but we had to say our final goodbyes and thanks, as we weren't joining the others for breakfast. We planned to leave by 6am to reach Heathrow for our British Airways flights to a Mexican honeymoon.

Everyone else rose later and had, by all accounts, a lovely morning meal without us. We'd fretted a bit, as unique occasions do have a habit of being ruinously expensive. As it happened, to accommodate and feed over twenty people, plus all the extras and many crates of wine and champagne, cost only £5,500. We were delighted, and upgraded our flights to first class as an extra gift to ourselves.

We spent New Year in Mexico City but during the next two weeks we travelled to both the Atlantic and Pacific coasts. I was especially keen to see some of the Mayan cities and temples, but this developed into an obsession. If you ever go to Mexico, I can recommend making the effort to see Tulum. It's an utterly stunning city overlooking the ocean but not entirely separate from the jungle.

The more I saw the more I wanted to see, even at the cost of spending time with Andrew. He was happy to lie on beaches, but I fidgeted and complained so it was just easier for him to let me go.

We stayed at a wonderful resort on Isla Mujeres for five days, which was possibly the best hotel room I've ever been in. We'd booked a junior suite but same-sex relationships are recognised and celebrated throughout Mexico, so we found ourselves upgraded to an enormous private villa. One morning, a spa therapist knocked at the door and offered whatever treatments we'd care to take, compliments of the management. At last, I thought, a good reason to have gone through with this whole partnership thing!

Andrew had a massage, but I opted for reflexology. I would have liked a massage too, but for those I've always preferred male therapists. (This has nothing to do with pressure points; it's just a personal preference.) But anyway, the reflexology was fantastically energising.

However, we did both have a paraffin hand peel, which was a truly novel experience. Both hands are immersed in hot paraffin, and then brought out while the oil hardens into a waxy coating around them. This stays on for a several minutes and is peeled off like a pair of rubber gloves. I was apprehensive as my hands were cleaned, but they emerged soft, glowing and feeling terrific. I now have a couple of these treatments a year, and I think of our honeymoon each time.

One thing we literally took from Mexico was a wooden Maya calendar. It's a metre across, intricately carved and now hangs on the wall above our bed. Maya calendars are spectacular items, works of supreme artistry in themselves.

My favourite gallery in the world is the Museum of Anthropology in Mexico City. We both visited twice for a total cost of £6. The grounds are enormous, with many buildings, housing different collections, set around a central courtyard. The main antiquities hall is mind-blowing, and a day could easily be wasted in just this one room seeing a fraction of the displays on offer.

The hall is dominated by a staggering Maya calendar on one wall. It's hewn from blocks of stone and stands eighteen metres tall but remains meticulously detailed. It is the very definition of awe-inspiring. Our honeymoon was the most luxurious trip I've ever taken but – just as I spent an hour staring at Picasso's *Guernica* when in Madrid – the sight of this calendar will remain my abiding memory.

Now that the law has changed, we will get married at some point but without a ceremony. A quick visit to the office, sign the papers and there we go. I had thought about live streaming the signing, as I've had a lot of requests from people who want to see it, but Andrew shuns all publicity so that idea's a non-starter.

I still campaign for equality though, and it annoys me when people are treated differently. Of course I wanted same-sex marriage, but what about opposite-sex civil partnerships? What about transgender and intersex individuals? The laws in this country are moving forward but have some way to go until they can justifiably be called equal and inclusive. I won't stop fighting until that day comes.

* * *

Dermot Murnaghan had exclusively hosted all the early *Eggheads* series. But after he moved from the BBC to Sky, it was announced that the presenter's role would be split between him and Jeremy Vine. I really didn't know what to think about this.

Jeremy was brilliant on the radio and with serious political topics but helming a light-hearted quiz show would be an entirely novel venture to him. He was also very religious, although not overtly so, and this reawakened old preconceptions in me. My views on organised religion have been effectively broadcast.

Although Dermot and I enjoyed a friendly respect, we'd never shared a single word outside of the studio. I feared my relationship with Jeremy would be strained from the outset and might deteriorate quickly.

I couldn't have been more spectacularly wrong. Jeremy is the kindest, most generous and considerate man I have met in television. His humour is contagious, his professionalism and skill are exemplary, and his evil wit is a glorious joy. After the very first block of filming together, he invited me round to his house. I met his stunning wife Rachel, a newsreader in her own right, and his two wonderful children. In his lounge, we stayed up past midnight as I taught him to play chess.

Obviously, it's incredibly rare that I'm wrong about anything, but on this occasion I was a complete prat. Jeremy Vine is a sheer delight and I can honestly say I'm honoured to know him.

Dermot remained in place for eighty shows, with Jeremy taking the next eighty. That was installed as the status quo, but I felt it couldn't last. It was clumsy, just for the sake of a sense of continuity. I wondered how and when it would be resolved.

Eggheads was now firmly established as one of the country's most popular and long-running programmes. Milestones started tumbling and, incredibly, we approached our 1,000th show. How on earth had that happened?

Eggheads books, a board game, various videogames and even pub games machines starting popping up everywhere. Two spin-off series of *Are You an Egghead?* brought Barry

Simmons and Pat Gibson onto the panel, which tremendously strengthened us as a team. Both are quizzers at the very highest level and, like Kevin Ashman, Pat is a world multi-champion. It was beginning to look as if no one could beat these Eggheads.

As part of the BBC's restructuring, we moved our recording circus up to Glasgow. I adore Scotland and was happy about the new location, though I'd have been equally at home in Salford, another prospect. This slashed production costs on an already cheap show; so as long as it defended the 6pm slot against all interlopers, its future was secure.

However, mine was anything but. I could no longer ignore impulses that had been gnawing and screaming at me for years. I wanted something substantial I could point to and proudly say, 'I did that!'

My forays into theatre had been pleasurable, but deep down I craved so much more. I'd need to make a tremendously risky sacrifice, with no guarantee of success and, in fact, an overwhelming likelihood of failure.

Nothing worthwhile is ever easy, and so, in 2011, after agonising over it for months, I made my momentous decision. I resigned from *Eggheads* to pursue my acting career fulltime.

11

SNOOKER (AND EXERCISE) LOOPY

I'm not a sports fan, as anyone who has seen me struggling with even the most basic football questions can attest. Snooker is different though, occupying a special place in my psyche after capturing my imagination at an early age. We've already established that I can't play, but I take a great deal of pleasure from spectatorship. I count myself as an expert on snooker history, especially the world championships, and apart from a handful of tennis matches, it's the only sport I've ever watched live.

I go to tournaments as much as my schedule and location allow. The Welsh Open was, until 2015, played only eight miles from my front door, which was splendidly convenient. I was at the event in February 2010 when Ivan from the media office noticed me. I told him what a huge fan I was and he suggested holding a quiz at that year's world championships. With no idea of what it might entail, I nodded very enthusiastically.

The resulting segments were aired in between the sessions of the first week, boasting the grand title *Snooker Eggheads*. I played individual rounds against John Virgo, Neal Foulds, Willie Thorne, John Parrott, Dennis Taylor and Terry Griffiths. This illustrious list of former players included three winners of the supreme title itself.

Michaela Tabb asked each of us ten questions, the twist being that they could choose a specialist subject whereas I had to answer on the world snooker championships. I comfortably won five of the mini-matches with only John Parrott besting me. I still haven't forgiven him and he knows it! It was great fun though, and I began to get to know some of the players personally.

When he burst onto the scene from nowhere in 2005 to become world champion, I took an instant dislike to Shaun Murphy. At twenty-two, he was the second youngest to win the tournament, but he was a chubby upstart and devout churchgoer. I didn't mind the former but was certain we wouldn't get on because of the latter.

Where this presumption came from I'm unsure, as I had no basis for believing I'd ever meet him. But then why do we adopt baseless opinions of others? It's an idiotic and immature approach, of which I was just as guilty as anyone. As I'd later learn with Jeremy Vine, it was pure ignorance to assume that someone of religious conviction would automatically reject me; I sincerely hope to never be so ill-informed again.

Shaun was such a total outsider that, even after taking the title, he remained miles away from the elite top-sixteen players. Without the automatic number one seeding for the holder, he would have to qualify for the next tournament with no assurance of getting through. He did, in fact, duly receive the top seeding, which was a little unfair to the world's number sixteen player of the time, who was himself plunged down into the qualifying rounds.

Gradually, I became a regular visitor to Sheffield every April to watch the biggest event in the snooker calendar, growing friendly with the players, officials and referees. As plenty of people do with footballers or pop stars, I get starstruck with men who hit brightly coloured balls around a table.

My introduction to the players' lounge at the Crucible was a daze of mute wonder. Stephen Hendry, Willie Thorne, Terry Griffiths and John Higgins were all there, but to them I was just some irrelevant television quizzer. John Parrott strode in, spotted me at once and came over with his hand extended. I muttered something inane about not needing to be told who he was, while staring at him with my very best wide-eyed Bambi impression. He'd been a long-standing team captain on *A Question of Sport*, so he had an affinity with quizzes and was an avid *Eggheads* viewer, which I took as a great compliment.

I slowly and timidly got to know the players, most of whom I really liked. Stuart Bingham is a particular delight and always smiling, an enviable talent I've never mastered. This draws people to him and quite rightly so, as he's a true gentleman.

It was Shaun I grew to know best, although it took a long time. We chatted casually at tournaments, and I started attending his matches, making a beeline to his table when available. As I had left *Eggheads*, I was free to appear on other programmes as a contestant. There was no ban technically in place while I was there, but it may have been seen as a conflict of interests.

A blatant demonstration of this was the ridiculous furore when Barry won the radio quiz *Brain of Britain* in 2013. The new BBC1 quiz, *Pointless*, was airing celebrity specials and I really wanted to take part. It was Twitter to the rescue: I messaged one of the stars, Richard Osman. I knew he was a big snooker fan too, so I offered him a quid pro quo: allow Shaun and I on the show, and I'd get him free passes to the upcoming world championships. We were ready to film in the studio within the month!

I've never done anything as nerve-wracking as *Pointless Celebrities*. Not because of the environment of the competition but simply because of my profile as a professional quizzer. My acting career hadn't gained traction yet, so to the public at large that's all I was. Therefore there was massive pressure on us to win.

During the briefings, the researcher asked me what two subjects I would least like to choose. The alarm bells in my brain went haywire and I considered lying. Then again, I assumed they already knew full well what my response would be. I honestly said, 'Music and football,' and my brow furrowed when she smiled, writing them down. Half an hour later, with the cameras rolling, the first two categories were music and football!

Shaun and I worked brilliantly as a team in those subjects. I rescued him on Eurovision, and he saved my blushes on footballers' wives. The head-to-head paired us against Ray Quinn and his future wife, Emma Stephens. From that juncture, I'm afraid my competitiveness took over, and I didn't allow Shaun another word. In the final, we had to choose between golf, which he preferred, and flags, which I wanted. We discussed it but had already made up our minds.

Shaun began, 'Look. We agreed that if we made it to the final, which we're very lucky to do after my answer in the first round...'

'Oh yes!' I interjected, rolling my eyes.

'...Then,' he continued, 'we'd go with whatever category you wanted.'

I turned to host Alexander Armstrong and said, 'We'll take flags please.'

The requirement was to name a national flag of three differently coloured parallel stripes but featuring no other symbols or markings at all. Within one second of the clock starting I blurted out, 'Chad!' and then waited.

All the questions in *Pointless* are asked to a hundred people before the show, and the contestants must then aim to provide a response the least number of people have offered. A point is scored for every person whose answer matches up so the best score will be the lowest, and the ideal score is the title of the show!

Alexander politely reminded us we could offer three answers, only one of which needed to be 'pointless' for us to win the jackpot. Rather cockily, but based on my experience, I commented we shouldn't need them as I was certain Chad would win. However, for the sake of it I added Russia and Netherlands to the list. They garnered seven and fourteen points respectively, but when the big fat zero appeared for Chad I jumped into the air, arms slung above my head.

In that moment, I felt neither happy for winning nor elated that our good cause would receive £2,500. I was overcome by a tidal wave of sheer relief that despite the huge burden of expectation, we'd done it. Imagine the reaction if a former Egghead had gone on *Pointless Celebrities* and not emerged victorious.

Our nominated charity was the Paul Hunter Foundation, set up in memory of the incredible snooker player who died crushingly young, five days before his twenty-eighth birthday. This wonderful organisation helps disadvantaged children to play sports and socialise, and I was so thrilled to be able to help in a small way. Paul was an amazing player, winning the Masters three times in four years, and is still missed by all who met him or saw him play.

Since then, Shaun and I have become good friends. Until very recently, however, I was still intimidated by him; even when he'd invited me along to an event, sorting out tickets and passes, I still hesitated to talk to him.

In 2015, he became only the tenth player ever to win snooker's triple crown of World Championship, UK Championship and Masters. Shortly afterwards, we had a long dinner and a talk. I think I'm almost at the point where I can relax with him now. It's only taken six years, which is pretty rapid for me.

My passion for snooker will always stay with me, and the opportunity to involve myself in its madcap whirl has been a great privilege. I've met so many lovely people, such as Michaela Tabb, who in 2009 became the first woman to referee the World Snooker Final, that superlative gentleman Ray Reardon and Steve Davis, who is quite simply a legend. Most remarkably for me, I don't say much when I meet these idols because I'm just struck dumb with awe and admiration.

*   *   *

I'd been a gym and fitness enthusiast for many years, and had even taken part in a small number of competitive running races. In 2009, I decided to go for the big one and entered the London Marathon. I just applied for the normal ballot, but my application was picked up and I was offered a media place.

This was a nice bonus, as those selected use a separate start line, restricted to about 200 people, that only joins the main race after half a mile. By then the crowd has thinned out, so slowing and getting jostled are less of a risk.

I had no idea how to prepare, so I did some casual road running but mainly focused on the treadmill. This was an enormous mistake, as I was to learn the hard way. Running outside is essential, as you learn to cope with the wind – especially when it's strong and directly in your face – and other weather conditions.

Now I actively try to run when it's cold, dark, wet or even snowing, to get used to everything nature can throw at me. That way, when it's actual race time, it's all so much easier than training.

In addition, race pace is always faster as you're pushed along by the adrenalin, crowd support and the impulse to finish that little bit sooner. Therefore, I don't merely concentrate on practising stamina and distance; I include time trials too.

One important point to bear in mind may sound counter-intuitive, but I promise you it's totally true: running a marathon is not twice as difficult as running a half-marathon; it's four or five times as difficult. Even the best athletes get drained and hit the wall, and this often happens early or in the middle of the second half. Once your body has used up all its sugar, it literally starts eating itself for energy. That's why sustained and sensible training is vital for such an immense challenge.

In 2009, I knew none of this and boy, did I pay for it.

My first assault on the London course was a nightmare. My preparation was patchy and ill thought-out, but I was enjoying the race up until the nineteen-mile mark. I wasn't doing too badly either, and had reached the distance in two and a quarter hours. Then I suddenly buckled under a searing pain in my right leg.

I saw a St John's Ambulance tent 100 metres ahead and limped towards it, almost dragging my limb behind me. I lay down, and after a brief examination the nurse told me I'd dislocated my knee. It had literally popped out of its socket, and my lower leg was just hanging there, unconnected to the rest of me.

With minimal warning, he clicked it back in – which was surprisingly free of the expected agony. Smiling, he proceeded to support and thoroughly bandaged my leg. After half an hour, it was repaired with a huge bulge of gauze and tape wrapped around it. He was advising on how I'd be ferried to the city centre to collect my bag, but I interrupted to thank him for his very kind help and started to get up.

He looked strangely at me as I insisted I wanted to finish the course. I'm not sure if his expression was one of admiration or relief that this madman was about to leave his tent, but he stood aside and I hopped off.

I was able to put pressure on the leg but nowhere near enough to run, so a bizarre combination of hopping and skipping ensued. I must have looked like a complete idiot to the runners of all shapes and sizes who were overtaking me, but embarrassment was the last thing I cared about.

I was even overtaken by a man wearing my favourite vest of the day: I read on his back the brilliant, 'Fat, fifty and in front of you.' My sole focus now was the finish line. The miles slowly clocked off, and I hobbled over the last timing board to complete the marathon in just over four hours and thirty-five minutes – which, incredibly, was still faster than the average. Since then, I've graduated to a higher competence of running, using road miles and my home gym to complement each other.

*　　*　　*

In August 2013, Andrew and I took a short but lovely break in Cyprus. The island itself didn't do much for me, and I found it a rather scruffy dumping ground for expats. Then again, it bore no comparison to a holiday we once booked to Greece.

For years I suffered with chronic hay fever. If you think this is only ever a mild condition, easily controllable and signified by a few light sniffles, allow me to disabuse you. For a small minority of people, myself included, it's utterly debilitating.

It tends to be cyclical and can occur at any age. For me, it materialised out of the blue when I was thirty-one and endured for ten years, before mercifully passing out of my system.

One year, the effects were so intense that I was bedridden, incapable of moving for six weeks, and I suffered the same incapacity the following year for a fortnight. I was unable to breathe through my nose, which was constantly blocked and severely painful. My eyes constantly itched and watered, and my throat was like rough sandpaper. Absolutely nothing worked and, as a last desperate resort, I travelled to Switzerland for an expensive course of steroids. Even that turned out to be miserably ineffective.

On one occasion, a block of *Eggheads* was scheduled during one of my attacks. This was in the early days of the show, when we still introduced ourselves, but I could barely speak. I went through several takes, and in the end we just had to settle for one that sounded like a cross between Darth Vader and Donald Duck.

After a brief consultation, the floor manager and producer went over to the challengers and asked them, very politely, if they would mind not picking me for a head-to-head. As my vocal cords were on strike, it would save me a burning effort and the office crew a lot of extra work. There was even talk of waiting a few days and getting me back in to dub all my answers!

The team very kindly agreed and offered their sympathies. I'm sure they'd never heard of a seasonal allergy being so severe, but I was in no position to talk to them about the subject. It seems to have left me now but, just to be safe, I generally spend the summer months at home where I'm used to, and immune from, the surrounding plants.

Anyway, we'd planned a wonderful Greek odyssey (see what I did there?), with three days in Athens to be followed by five in Thessaloniki. We arrived at our funky city centre hotel, which rather wonderfully had convertible Minis as reception desks. A walk around the Acropolis museum was succeeded by a superb lunch of marinated feta cheese and salads at a roadside taverna. The city was very brown with few trees, but incredibly dusty, so we were grateful when the heavens opened during our meal.

My gratitude was short-lived as the rain set me off, leaving me in the throes of the worst reaction I've ever had. We'd been in Greece for four hours and I was already in agony. I lasted until evening and then begged Andrew to get me out of there. We rushed back to the hotel, but my eyes were streaming and I was yelping in pain. The schedules were checked, but we'd left it too late to catch any of the remaining flights back to the UK. The next available was at 8am, so I could do nothing but wait.

I'm not a good patient. I spent the entire night sweating and cursing, all the while wandering around the hotel in ever-deepening discomfort. Andrew, of course, slept soundly, but I became increasingly vocal and angry at the invisible specks of pollen that had felled me.

We couldn't get to the airport early enough, booking new flights back to London. I took a business-class seat and fortunately, besides one other person, had the cabin to myself. I would have been intolerable in economy, with masses of other people.

The car valets at Heathrow were thrown into a fuss when Andrew called them upon landing, but our car was waiting for us after we'd passed customs. After a drive of two hours with the air conditioning turned up to the full Arctic, we arrived home with my nipples so hard they could have cut glass. I went straight to bed and stayed there for three days, until I recovered sufficiently to be able to move about again.

With all the changes and non-refundable hotels, nineteen hours in Greece had cost us £3,500. Still, I got to see a couple of nice statues and had some lovely cheese – so all in all, it was well worth it.

This brings me back to our holiday in Cyprus. We stayed at a pleasant hotel in Pissouri, adjacent to a restaurant serving the most delicious coated halloumi cheese. Don't confuse this with the rubbery stodge we put up with over here; this was soft, stringy and melt-in-the-mouth. If I ever go back to this part of the world, I need to be somewhere with a lot of gyms as I'll be on an all-cheese diet!

Driving back to the resort one day, I asked Andrew to drop me off at the top of a hill by the famous RAF Akrotiri base. This would leave me with nine miles to go and, as he wanted to pop down to look at a nearby beach, it might make for a nice run.

In fact, it turned out to be heavenly. I ran for a little over an hour, passed by only four cars in the warm, friendly sunshine. I got back to our villa in advance of Andrew, which was irritating as he still had the key. I scrambled over the fence, stripped off and plunged into our private pool, having seconds to spare to shake off and leap onto a sun lounger before he made his bemused entrance. I've run thousands of miles in training, but those were the best nine miles ever.

Running is now a very important part of my life. I'd like to return to somewhere like Cyprus, or perhaps Majorca, and have a running holiday. The problem is that none of my friends possess the necessary fitness levels, so it'd have to be a solitary break. Not that I necessarily mind, but it's nice to have some company now and then.

*   *   *

In 2014, I entered my fourth London Marathon, despite very little training and suffering a freak accident. Four days before the race, I was on the treadmill at a gym in Covent Garden, completing a long run. I switched off the machine, allowed the belt to come to a standstill, turned around and promptly fell off the end, twisting my right ankle. I limped very painfully to the changing room; after a shower and five minutes in the sauna, I found I couldn't walk.

This was unchanged throughout the next few days; with forty-eight hours to go, my chances of competing looked slim. However, with nursing and gentle massage it improved; by the Sunday morning I could jog – but nothing more.

I didn't want to withdraw, so I turned up at the start line as usual and set off at the gun. I could feel tenderness with every step, but have a natural aversion to taking tablets. Unless it's unbearable, no discomfort is ever worth me taking a painkiller, so I just dealt with it and carried on.

I had no idea what I was expecting. With this on top of my lack of practice, crossing the finish line in 3.16.09 was a considerable surprise. I was at once taken to one side and told I'd won the celebrity race, which was quite a shock!

In the media area, over 100 competitors had been given special trackers to carry around the course. I'd unexpectedly come home ahead of a variety of sportsmen, including Steven Gerrard who was second, about ten minutes behind.

I was interviewed live by Jonathan Edwards, and was so euphoric that I blurted out a very bold statement: I proclaimed that I'd return the next year, not only to win the celebrity race but also to break the magical barrier of three hours.

As it transpired, media place demand for 2015 was so high that it had to be opened to a ballot, as is the case with the standard race start. I was lucky enough to be accepted, but only, I imagine, on the strength of my 2014 showing and extravagant claims thereafter.

As I write this, the fateful day is almost upon us, but I'm confident of keeping my word. I've got into the habit of getting up at 6am and going for a run before breakfast. My times, and my waistline, have been reducing steadily. This is another of those big personal ambitions: if I don't put in the effort, you can be damn sure no one else will do it for me!

* * *

My 2015 New Year's resolution was to finally get the body I've always wanted. My marathon training has indisputably helped towards that. I have broad shoulders, but gaining muscle is of no interest. Being slim and toned is what I aspire to. My waist has gone from seventy-five to seventy-three centimetres, and my weight from sixty-nine to sixty-five kilos. Not too shabby for half a year's effort. My main problem is, and always will be, that I eat total rubbish.

Believe me, if I could, I'd live on pizza. In fact, I tried it for six months in 2010 and, as enjoyable as it was, there were unpleasant side effects. My daily diet was two croissants in the morning and a large pizza mid-afternoon. I was still exercising, but this didn't yet include running, so I put on two kilos and my complexion erupted.

I reluctantly gave it up and pizza is now a rare, although much dreamt of, luxury. I'm grateful I live in the middle of nowhere, as none of the fast food places deliver to my house. Both Pizza Hut and Domino's are eight miles away in opposite directions, but neither condescends to come here. Can you imagine what size I'd be if they did?

I'm worried I may not be able to maintain this level of exercise once the challenge of the marathon has passed, assuming that I achieve my targets. Mind you, actually getting into the habit of early morning runs is far more difficult than maintaining it. My all-consuming vanity should give me a push anyway, so let's be positive and say I'll be able to continue.

If I had the facilities, inclination and partners to play other sports, I'm sure I'd enjoy them. Tennis, baseball and even rugby have appeal, but I have to balance this against my desire to live in the wilderness.

Unless I'm working, I have an aversion to cities now, so the solitude invariably wins out. The loneliness of the long distance runner it is, then.

12

WHAT'S NEXT?

My personal life was happy but my professional life had stalled. I'd made a lot of contacts and even dared to call some of them friends, but I was failing to make the big push. I'd left a well-paid, high profile job to chase my dream and had to believe that it wasn't in vain. I never thought it a mistake because it was the right decision at the time and, as we know, I don't do regrets. To be successful within my chosen field I had to take some sort of risk, but I'd taken an almighty one.

In late 2012, via Twitter, I got to know a composer called Scott Morgan who invited me to join him for a reading of a new musical he'd written, called *Geek!* It was an outrageous high-school piece but unlike anything seen previously. It didn't just push the envelope; it ripped it open and then vomited on the contents.

We discussed the concept and I agreed to produce it at the Tristan Bates Theatre in Covent Garden. This is a wonderful little space of about sixty seats, adjacent to the Actor's Centre. I didn't know it at the time but this venue would come to play a very big part in my acting career.

Unfortunately, costs spiralled out of control very quickly, as we had a cast of sixteen, a live band of three and an annoyingly complicated set. I managed to secure the wonderful Ewen Macintosh to play the headmaster, and I took the role of the alcoholic, nymphomaniac teacher Ms Axel. We were an instant hit and people reported wetting themselves with laughter. One prominent review insisted, 'Forget *Book of Mormon*, *Geek!* is now the most offensive show in London!' I adored this accolade so much that I added it to our flyers.

We risked, and got away with, scenes that might once have been considered unthinkable. In one scene, I staggered onto stage in a lace basque, chasing a naked boy while my hand was thrust inside an inflated sex doll – you know, all the typical stuff of West End farce!

We ran for four weeks, the last of which was a complete sell-out. Customers moaned that they couldn't get tickets, but we were unable to extend and, frankly, they should have come earlier in the run.

Geek! was a fantastic experience but also very expensive. Although I gained invaluable acting and producing credits, I personally lost about £10,000 from it. I'd always been prepared for some sort of financial hit, but the scale came as a juddering shock.

I auditioned for plays I wanted and turned down some

I didn't. I continued with singing, but my enthusiasm had waned considerably since my *Grease* disappointment. Besides, I'd now chosen my path; more dramatic roles were where my real interest lay.

But I was at a loss about how to make that breakthrough. Of course, this was no different to innumerable aspiring actors, and I was far less deserving than many of them. They trained for several years, holding down multiple jobs to make ends meet, all for that tiny chance of the limelight. I was just a schmuck with a big mouth, who landed a television job out of nowhere because of it. My life had been nothing more than a series of lucky breaks. Serendipity realised this, and readied itself to intervene once more.

In early 2012, with no warning, Rob, the executive producer of *Eggheads*, suddenly texted to see how I was. I'd had no contact with anyone at all from the programme for eighteen months, so this was most unexpected. I love Rob and was honoured that he was a guest at our civil partnership ceremony.

But this made me a little suspicious. I replied honestly, saying I was finding my fledgling career tough, but not unexpectedly so. It would just be a case of battling on, waiting for that one chance, that one role to catapult me forwards.

He suggested meeting for lunch and my self-preservation instincts kicked in. I never like revealing too much to people, in case it gives them an advantage or something to use against me. Just because I'm paranoid doesn't mean they aren't actually out to get me.

I played my cards close to my chest, telling him I'd be in

London in a week and could probably find time then. We met and had an inoffensive few minutes shooting the breeze, until I got impatient. I've never been very good at small talk or playing games, so I asked him straight out why he'd wanted to get together.

I'd had discussions with other channels, recorded a couple of pilots and even been approached by another quiz show in the interim. As these weren't secrets, word had undoubtedly got around.

Rob asked me if I'd be interested in returning to *Eggheads*. As flattered as I was, I flat-out said no. I will admit to a little *schadenfreude* here; I wasn't entirely displeased to think the show might be slipping a little in the ratings without me. I in no way wanted to it to fail, but it's always nice to have a small ego boost now and again.

He then began hinting at other projects, and I had to push him to get to the point. It transpired that another *Eggheads* spin-off was in the pipeline and they wanted me to front it. The plan was for only one series but it would help the main programme, on the condition I was willing to rejoin.

I felt privileged to be faced with such a lovely dilemma, but asked for time to think about it. To be perfectly honest, I might have agreed immediately, but I was still waiting to hear about two other options. One was a quiz on a satellite network, the other a play in Germany. The injustices of show business were never more clearly demonstrated than in these two cases.

In the first, the programme was commissioned and I was offered the job. Then the commissioning editor went off on holiday and resigned without coming back, having decided she wanted to be an author instead. The new man came on board and, without hesitation, cancelled all her outstanding projects in order to make his own mark.

The second was even worse; the casting called for a man of slightly Mediterranean appearance – early forties, slim, athletic, dark hair, green eyes, with a baritone voice – who was a fluent German speaker. Now, call me cynical but I don't think they would have been inundated with applicants who ticked every one of those boxes. I genuinely did but received a deafening silence in return. What does a boy have to do to get a break in this town?

After a little more hesitation, I agreed to resume working with 12 Yard and we moved on with plans for *Revenge of the Egghead*. This was to be hosted by Jeremy Vine; I may not even have accepted if he hadn't been in place. A more confrontational and sarcastic tone was required, but Jeremy and I can play off each other very well, and I think we ended up with an excellent show.

Five contestants started each day to build up a prize fund, while I tried to catch each out and eliminate as many as I could. The final round winner would be whoever could answer the most questions correctly, whether it was the remaining players combined or me. Generally it was expected to be me but, unusually, my nerves were a big factor.

Revenge was definitely a high-pressure situation for everyone taking part, but the majority was heaped on my shoulders. This told in the early episodes as I only won three of the first five. I was reminded of the weight of expectation from *Pointless Celebrities*, and how it had almost affected my performance.

After twenty-one games, I only emerged as victor in a

miserable thirteen and was feeling a little downhearted. The final three days of filming would produce nine shows, and I'd have to win eight of them to end the series with a respectable seventy per cent success rate.

I cut back a little on the witty retorts and snappy comebacks, putting all my effort into avoiding silly, costly errors. I ensured there was still plenty of material for the final edit, so the quality never suffered, but my competitive nature really kicked in.

In the final tally I did manage to win eight of the last batch, so I totalled twenty-one wins against only nine losses, which everyone was happy with. Rob and the other producers commented, once we'd wrapped, on how anxious they'd been after the first couple of days. Anything close to a fifty-fifty win rate would have been disastrous, but fortunately the whole crew came through to create something fantastic.

Revenge of the Egghead was popular and critically acclaimed, attracting enthusiastic reviews. One in the *Daily Mail* read, 'CJ has the brains to match his swagger.' For some reason I quite liked that.

I was now entrenched back in the main show, but it was lacking a vital factor. Dave Rainford had been brought in following my departure, well known as 'Tremendous Knowledge Dave' from radio stations around the Manchester area. He is a lovely guy and a recognised sports expert, a great addition to the line-up.

However, we'd lost the greatest female quizzer in the world, as Daphne had retired. After a decade on the panel, she felt the moment was right and stepped down, representing a great loss both to *Eggheads* and the world of television.

But we were soon to have our numbers swollen to eight by the addition of Lisa Thiel. She had been a member of a winning trio on *Revenge*, and received an invitation to join the very next day, while shopping in a supermarket!

Lisa has been a wonderful breath of fresh air, and I believe this is critical for any long-running event, onscreen or not. People may enjoy something comfortable and repetitive, but eventually they'll get bored. Introducing new characters, hosts, tweaks to the rules and so on are proven techniques across the field. They retain the interest of the current audience while hopefully attracting new fans.

Eggheads has employed all of these and the proof is in the pudding. After a dozen years, it stubbornly retains its place in the schedules and the public's affections.

So I was back on television fulltime. Surprisingly, because of all the repeats, it wasn't fully understood that I'd even left! My screen absence probably only lasted seven months and, somewhat depressingly, I may not have been missed at all.

I'm not daft enough to dismiss a renewed national profile as irrelevant, but it was yet to lead to that one theatre role I craved so much. Fortunately, a friend was about to introduce me to it.

I'd met the aspiring director Dan Phillips in 2012. He was studying and teaching at the Mountview Academy drama school in north London, and it was here that I went to see *Sisters*, one of his productions. To be honest, I didn't much care for the piece or – lead actor Hamish Colville aside – the performances, but the direction was beautiful.

It's difficult for me now to watch plays without my

professionally critical eye dissecting every nuance. I find it detracts from the sheer thrill of the theatre, and I often wonder if this is why so many critics are nasty just for the sake of it. Perhaps they lack the capacity to engage in what they're reviewing – whether it be acting, writing, painting, cooking or whatever else – and so they must rubbish those who do. I'm gratified to see that this subgenre of criticism is dying out, as the demand for honest and constructive reviews takes over.

There were aspects of *Sisters* I found fascinating, and all were of Dan's own design. Very rarely will you meet someone you feel you simply have to work with, but I'd done just that. We met for lunch soon after and he revealed he'd always wanted to direct something by Harvey Fierstein – coincidentally one of my very favourite playwrights, and perhaps the most popular alive today.

Fierstein's plays and musicals are performed worldwide, but his reputation was built on startlingly modern pieces written in the 1980s. A gay, Jewish actor and writer growing up in New York as the AIDS crisis was starting to impact, he was hugely influenced by the fight that the gay community found itself up against, and the devastating effect of the disease on everyone around him.

The seminal *Torch Song Trilogy* set the scene; he followed it with his *Safe Sex Trilogy* and other plays, which would have been starkly shocking to even the most liberal audiences of the time. His skill was to interweave pathos and humour, allowing a flicker of hope to shine through. AIDS is not the most naturally comedic of theatrical themes, but I doubt many people left his performances feeling depressed. That wouldn't have been Fierstein's aim, or a particularly effective way of getting his message across.

Even today, enormous stigmas and fears endure about HIV and AIDS. These are just diseases like any other. We're all aware of the main ways in which the virus is transmitted, but some bigots ludicrously argue that because infection usually stems from consensual sexual activity, free treatment should be denied.

Please don't leave me in a locked room with anyone who propounds this viewpoint, as I won't be responsible for my actions. Should we deny treatment to many cancer sufferers who are smokers, overeaters and so on? Of course not, and AIDS is no different.

In my time volunteering for various charities, I've been with several people as they've died. Can you imagine being shunned and ignored just because you have a microscopic virus inside you? I can't comprehend a worse experience than dying alone in a corner with every person refusing to touch you, and yet this is a daily reality the world over.

I've held, cuddled and lain next to several men, and one woman, as their bodies have let go. I refuse to allow anyone to be scared or lonely in the final moments of life. I've taken a lot of criticism for this, usually from people who have no knowledge or experience of AIDS, but this book isn't the place to detail those conversations. Suffice to say, my responses have not been restrained.

I am deeply loved, but many of those terminally ill from AIDS-related ailments are not. I for one won't stand by and ignore them, and neither should anyone else.

Bear this terrifying fact in mind: today, in 2015, nearly

one per cent of the entire human population is HIV positive. Until a cure is found for this pandemic, it is our moral responsibility to take care of those less fortunate. We're all members of humankind; the very word itself should say it all.

Torch Song Trilogy had recently been performed in London but the *Safe Sex Trilogy* had never received a professional production in Britain. We rejected the first part as too short and outdated, but the second and third, *Safe Sex* and *On Tidy Endings*, were fantastic. The roles of Ghee and Arthur massively appealed, especially the latter in the longer, more intense piece. We resolved to stage the plays and the Tristan Bates seemed the perfect venue.

Both plays only totalled ninety-five minutes in running time, but as with *Deathtrap,* I had the bulk of the lines. Although *Safe Sex* included a great monologue for my character, *On Tidy Endings* is the most satisfying production I've acted in. The piece is essentially a two-hander between a woman whose husband, Colin, had revealed he was gay and HIV positive after many years of marriage, and Arthur, Colin's partner for his final three years.

It demanded a whole range of moods, and Arthur was an emotionally draining part to play every day. After its forty-five minutes, I was exhausted. Nevertheless, I adored every second and have rarely felt more at home than I did on that stage during our run of four weeks.

The audiences grew but, as is the way with the fringe, even in the heart of the West End, the last week sold out and people complained. I had little sympathy with those who expressed dissatisfaction at the dearth of tickets. The glowing four- and five-star reviews were published during week one, so there was plenty of time.

I kept costs down as much as was realistic, but actually lost even more money due to paying professional rates. My knock came in at a shade under £11,000, yet I didn't begrudge a single penny. For the experience, the credit, the reviews, it was worth it all. Maybe the most valuable thing to me was a seismic shift in popular and professional opinion of what I could do, and a new appreciation of my acting.

Mind you, given the choice, I'd have preferred to achieve all that without losing the cash!

Eggheads ploughed on, accompanied in my schedule by pantomime and other occasional gigs, like acting as Master of Ceremonies for concerts or charity events. I wrote and hosted quizzes around the country, but nothing really enthused me in the way *On Tidy Endings* had done. I needed that buzz back, and it was to come from a rather unusual direction.

I spoke to Ed Greenberg about the feedback from *The Renata Road*. We discussed attempting a full-length feature film based on the short, despite knowing it would be a massive and costly undertaking. Ed collaborated with various writers to produce a script he considered worthy of the project. I read it and was, for want of a better word, gobsmacked.

If this made it to the big screen, it would be unlike anything that had been seen before. Dialogue was kept to a minimum except for a small number of pivotal scenes, and the whole film revolved around the unnamed central character. As with the short, the feature would be a dark psychological thriller where a lone stranger, played by me, checks into a claustrophobic hotel inhabited by mysterious guests and staff. I was set to appear in all but four scenes, which would make for a very intense and emotionally draining workload.

Squeezing every margin, we intended to make it on a shoestring budget not exceeding £15,000, which for a cinematic movie is almost unheard of. Let me put that in perspective for you: it's the same amount James Cameron spent to make one second of *Titanic*!

Ed was to direct and I would take the lead role, as well as being executive producer. The critical priority was to raise the money, so we looked at a number of avenues. I committed £5,000 and we launched a crowd-funding appeal, which garnered a further £6,500. A friend gave us £1,000 and we reached our target after I hosted two large quizzes.

One of these was in a hall in central Manchester, but the other was at a hotel in Lytham proposed as the main filming location. This took place in mid-2013, and was notable for a random meeting. During the evening, a young man in a shirt that would embarrass even me on *Eggheads* sidled up quietly to say hello.

I replied in kind and it took a minute of him standing there, while I awkwardly tried to get on with things, for the light bulb to go on. His name was Dan and I realised then that we'd been chatting on Twitter for quite some time.

For me, social media is just that. I use it to engage with my fans on issues I find compelling. I don't understand celebrities who simply use it to hawk their own products, or to seek validation by only replying to other high-profile figures. Interact with the people who put you where you are, for goodness' sake!

Dan had mentioned he might attend, as he'd been playing

in a poker tournament in the area and was a quizzing addict. After the evening had concluded, we talked briefly before going our separate ways.

For some reason, I found myself thinking about Dan despite superficially having nothing in common at all. He was a twenty-nine-year-old night-shift supermarket worker from Scunthorpe, whose pastimes seemed to be poker, copious amounts of alcohol and mature ladies. None of these feature high on a list of CJ's proclivities, so there was no discernible reason why we'd ever get along.

However, later in the week I called him to say hello, and before long had invited him down to Wales for the weekend. We clicked immediately; he was so relaxed and amiable, once he'd got over his initial reticence and shyness. And I, for the first time in my whole life, had a best friend.

There's no subject that's off limits between Jamie Chapman Dixon and I, but seeing Dan far more regularly gives him that slight edge; sorry, Jamie. I've even got him using moisturisers and applying for television quiz shows. My work here is nearly complete!

We've tried and failed to understand why it works with us, but when you meet someone with whom you have an instant rapport, my advice is to go with the flow. Dan and I have the sort of friendship where we can do anything together without the need for words. We can sit quietly for hours or impulsively jump up, drive to the airport and pop over to Amsterdam for the day.

That's the kind of love I never thought I'd have, but with him it's easy. I have wonderful friends, an amazing home life and an enviable career. I've now got a best friend to top it all off. No matter what glittering accolades are destined to be showered on *The Renata Road* – and if it's received anywhere near as well as the short from which it's expanded, I'll consider that a great success - meeting Dan might be the most important consequence of the whole film, for me personally.

The other nine roles in the movie were cast and filming was set for January 2014. It was likely we'd have to do pickups further down the line, once the primary block was out of the way, but three days were pencilled in for April. It would actually warrant a full extra week, delayed until June, as we needed a complicated two-room set built from scratch.

The schedule was severe, and I do not know how Ed coped. A couple of the actors (myself not amongst them, I hasten to add, as I was conscious of my executive producer position) were rather difficult and argumentative. Low salary is no excuse for low standards, and no justification to cause problems, as everyone's in the same boat.

Ed displayed patience and tolerance well beyond anything I'd be capable of. We had very long days and had to function around a working hotel and its guests. For three consecutive days we were called on set for 7am, and worked straight through for twenty-three hours. This was method acting at its finest, as the actors were meant to look stressed and dishevelled by this point.

The poor crew, however, were not, and I must mention Craig Priestley, who worked harder than I've seen anyone work in my life. I'm not even sure what his job officially was, because he did everything. He built sets, carried lights, positioned everything, fetched coffee, sorted out microphones and countless other tasks besides. He was a highly skilled technician but preferred to do everything himself to ensure it was done properly.

My respect for him grew every day and I often offered to help, but Ed told me to keep my place. This was quite right and proper, as Craig, overworked as he was, could manage, and I had my own job to concentrate on.

The most full-on three and a half weeks of my career (so far!) ended, and we had the majority of the film in the can. Further scenes would be added, but that was the opening round complete. Post-production is the most arduous part of filmmaking, but, because virtually all our budget had been used, we were in no position to pay anyone to do it quickly. Colouring, editing, syncing and all the meticulous detail of getting a movie right now began, but it was going to take months to complete.

As an actor wanting to specialise in more serious roles, there was one gaping hole in my CV. My credits had been slowly building, and I had an impressively varied array of roles to my name. The omission was nonetheless conspicuous by its absence, so I took the plunge and auditioned for a couple of Shakespeare plays.

To make it worse, they were two I hadn't the faintest idea about. The Lazarus Theatre was staging *Troilus and Cressida* alongside *Coriolanus* as part of the Camden Fringe at – you've guessed it – the Tristan Bates. My expectations weren't high, as I've never been a fan of Shakespeare and feel ill at ease with the way his work is academically idolised. That wasn't his intention when writing it; he wanted entertainment for the masses, but now it's been co-opted by semantic snobs and almost taken away from the very audiences it was intended for.

I'd had little enough faith in my aptitude to cope with the two open workshop auditions, but as they were texts I was neither familiar with nor understood, my confidence was reduced to zero. This wasn't helped when I found myself surrounded by experienced and skilled actors, led by the hard-working and knowledgeable director Ricky Dukes. He claimed he saw a willingness in me, as I eagerly portrayed a five-year-old boy playing with soldiers at his request.

I have no problem doing anything on stage and this was relatively mild, but it was enough to spark some interest in him. Two days later Ricky emailed and offered me a role in each play. Thersites in *Troilus and Cressida* is a relatively small but pivotal role, but Menenius in *Coriolanus* was a very major character. I don't know if I was more elated or petrified.

I found it incredibly difficult to learn the lines. My utter lack of empathy with the characters or dialogue massively hindered my development. Some actors tell me this is my problem, and I must work to eradicate it; I tell them they must sod off.

I confess I didn't like the way the company worked in rehearsals. Far too much time, in my opinion, was given over to getting to know the space, understanding our bodies, our voices and each other. I accept these methods work for other performers, but they leave me cold and I certainly wasn't alone in my view.

It reminded me of a drama lesson from when I was much younger. The teacher, a waif-like hippy of a woman, asked the children to stand around the room and imagine they were trees. We had to convey the sunlight on our branches, the gentle swirling of the breeze around our leaves, the minute nibbling of the insects on our bark, the sound of animals in the distance, and the water in the atmosphere, drawing up through our roots. She said the key was to do it all without moving a single muscle. But I did move, walking straight past her and out of the door. I'd see enough wooden acting in my time, but being asked to be a tree was a ridiculous step too far.

I only fully got Shakespeare's lines into my head two days before we opened. I tried to inhabit the roles but they were problematic, especially our abridged *Troilus and Cressida*, which I simply didn't understand. The plays went well and received good reviews, with a couple even singling me out.

But there were far more talented actors alongside me, who were relaxed with the material and positively shone on stage. I pushed myself but could never quite reach my goals. I now have Shakespeare credits on my CV, but they brought me no real satisfaction and this is down to nothing more than personal taste. From what I've done in my acting career, I find I'm more attuned to twentieth-century writing, especially American and Russian drama. I connect to the characters more intimately, which is essential to playing them convincingly.

I won't again be in a position where I accept a job just because the credit or profile (you'll notice I'm not mentioning the salary) is enticing. For example, it may be a popular programme, but I've declined *Celebrity Masterchef* as I can barely make toast. I have my price, of course, but would have to think very seriously before opening myself up to ridicule. I've had plenty of experience with prostitution, and I'm not in a rush to metaphorically revisit those days. I don't have too much self-respect, but what remains is pretty expensive to buy.

* * *

I failed to secure a pantomime for winter 2014, even though I was offered not one but two. Both fell through, with the second collapsing too late for another role to become available. It was a relief to be free of the punishing schedule for one holiday period, but I rather missed the hustle, the fun and the money. But then a dinner meeting in late November, with my friend Jack Thorpe-Baker, persuaded me it was really a blessing in disguise. I hadn't known Jack very long and, as seems to be quite common now, I'd first started chatting to him through Twitter. He'd been in theatre since childhood and was a very accomplished dancer and choreographer.

If I wanted to be in the frame for bigger roles he explained, I had to increase my visibility and writing an autobiography was the best way to do it. Immediately I reverted to my default position and stated my reasons for not wanting to but he was quite insistent, and over the course of the evening convinced me I just had to get on and write. My friends knew what my life had been like, but even Dan and Jamie had only scratched the surface. If I were to do this, it would be a major enterprise even though I find writing very easy.

I put my words down without any definite structure or

plan in mind. Although I made no notes, I tried to stay in a roughly chronological order but inevitably leapt around, tying in different times and topics. I personally find this the most interesting way, as a straight linear storyline can be a bit tedious. I hope it's the same for most other people but, if not, this book is probably immensely frustrating!

The more I turned it over, the more I realised Jack was right. I'd reached an impasse, and to surmount it I either needed a spectacularly lucky break or a new line of attack. Millions hope for the former, but I numbered amongst the few who had the latter as a viable option.

I talked it over with Andrew, slept on it and texted Jack to say he was correct. I marked off five months to complete the book and to train for the London Marathon. Very reluctantly, I decided not to apply for theatrical roles during that time. I even stopped checking the daily casting calls, as I knew full well I'd be tempted.

If I put my name forward and auditioned, the worst outcome would be the offer of a part. There would follow the heartbreaking dilemma of whether to turn down a dream role and damage my reputation in professional circles.

There is nobody, especially in the theatre, who wants to have his or her time wasted, so my complete absence was the only choice. Apart from *Eggheads* and a few small quiz and charity gigs, December 2014 to April 2015 would consist of nothing but writing and training.

My attempt to break the three hours' barrier for the London Marathon had been playing on my mind for ages. I'd started exercising to reach this incredibly hard goal. But my regime was nowhere near as intense as would be required, and taking a few months off might bring me, literally, up to speed.

I was ready for a mammoth endeavour but wasn't sure if I, as an amateur of forty-five, would be able to achieve a very high level of athletic success. If I did it, I'd finish in the top five per cent of the field and virtually everyone ahead of me would be a professional or regular club runner. My only basis for comparison was my 2014 time, when I was undertrained and injured. I started to believe that, with dedication, it might just be doable.

I trained hard, waking at 6am to go out running within an hour. I bought specialist running clothes, as the cold weather is a powerful deterrent and I couldn't afford to waste any days, never mind weeks. I think this is a reason many runners are unprepared for the London race. They prefer to stay huddled in their warm duvets rather than go out into the cold.

By the end of January, my habitual five miles was no longer enough and I was building the runs up to eight or ten. I entered the Brighton and Reading half-marathons at the end of February and March respectively, as warm ups. They would be my first competitive races since London 2014, so it was vital to test and time myself. My main fear was injury, but I invested in the proper training gear and shoes. This built endurance and gave me the best chance of protecting my body.

I desisted from running on my treadmill but walked on it for hours every day to maintain base fitness. I worked on flexibility and all the tiny muscles we rarely use, but that nevertheless get a thorough workout during a long race.

One aspect frequently overlooked by casual distance runners is chest strength. Over half or full marathons, the arms are pumping so often that it's like thousands of gentle chest presses. These add up, and if you can't push forward with your arms then running, especially up an incline, is severely limited. Whole body fitness is essential, so training has to be more than a boring pounding of the streets.

I'd love to be able to find a regular running partner but, living miles from anywhere, it's never going to happen. I don't like the idea of driving ten miles to my 'local' running club for an evening, and then driving back again. I tried it once and, although I was slower than their top two members, I was much faster than everyone else, so I ended up running alone anyway. I can do that near my home and save myself twenty miles' worth of petrol.

On 21 February 2015, Andrew and I headed down to Brighton to stay with our friends Martin and Helen. I get such a rush of adrenalin the night before a race that it feels like I'm nervous, but I know it's just excited anticipation.

As a competitor with one of the faster predicted finishing times, I began the half-marathon very near the front – not that this really matters. A timing chip doesn't register until it crosses the start line, but the advantage of being one of the first is that the crowd is initially much thinner, allowing the runner to get into a free pace more quickly.

We set off and, as always, hundreds of people came shooting past me. This is a rookie mistake. I gladly let them all go and continued at my own pace. I was self-aware enough to know how fast to run, despite my lack of a watch or any timers along the course.

This is one great feature of the London Marathon. Every mile marker has a clock in it, so accurate pacing is eminently possible. Over twenty-six miles this is very useful, but at half-distance an experienced runner knows what to do.

Over the race, I stuck to my plan and reeled in all the over-enthusiastic starters as they flagged and slowed. My aim was to finish within ninety minutes and in the top five per cent of the field.

The first I achieved with twenty-four seconds to spare, which may not sound a lot but was right on target for what I wanted. The second I missed by an agonisingly tiny margin of 0.1 per cent, but placing at 388 out of 7,731 starters was not bad at all in the lead-up to Reading and London. The big day was only nine weeks away, and I still had an awful lot of hard work to get through.

A month later, although I shaved a few seconds off my personal best at the Reading half-marathon, I wasn't happy with the race organisation. Staggered start times for different sections meant I wasn't able to properly time myself, as the pacemaker I wanted to stay ahead of started minutes before me.

It was a very strange state of affairs. Still, it was good competitive practice and my training continued, including a twenty-seven mile run with a fortnight to go before the big day.

When Jonathan Edwards interviewed me after the 2014 race, my vest was drenched with blood trickling from my left nipple. For 2015, blood could have been pouring from every orifice, with me screaming in agony, but my determination to force my aching body towards that finish line would not be dimmed. Pain is temporary but glory is permanent, and I would fight through one to achieve the other.

I approached race day with four aims, only one of which I thought I was likely to achieve. Firstly and most importantly, I desperately wanted to beat the magical three-hour barrier. Secondly, I hoped to win the celebrity race for the second consecutive year. This was going to be difficult, as Formula One driver Jenson Button was in the field and he's an experienced triathlete with impressive marathon times behind him, so my third ambition was to at least finish ahead of him. Finally, the most difficult target was to beat the celebrity record set by Nell McAndrew in 2012 of 2.54.39.

I thought that, if I could be successful in all of these, I might be able to market myself as an ultra-fit and intelligent celebrity. Perhaps it's a niche market, but I'd rather be the big fish in a tiny pond, enjoying all of the scraps, than a small fish in an ocean, trying to grab the occasional nibble.

My manager Steve Mottershead and I had a plan to make the most of any publicity to secure work, so the months of effort were going to be worth it. I'd met Steve several years earlier when he and multi-world champion darts player Phil Taylor were contestants on Eggheads. Although their team lost comfortably, I had the honour of beating Phil in an arts and books round while Steve beat Kevin, the world's best quizzer, on entertainment. I'm only telling this here because Steve is so reluctant to tell this story. Honestly, he barely mentions it two or three times an hour now so you'd really never know.

Sunday, 26 April 2015 had arrived; as did I, nervously, at the green-start media tent. My bag had been carefully and methodically packed, so I slowly went through my routine, nibbled an energy bar and pinned my number to my vest.

I was running to support Shooting Star Chase Hospices, a small charity that provides care and support for children with life-shortening conditions. I'd got to know about their wonderful work through Jamie and his mother Nicole, both of whom worked for them. I'd already taken part in a few theatrical events with Jamie, but wanted to do something a little more significant.

I always prefer to raise funds and awareness for smaller charities, as they sometimes get lost in a sea of bigger organisations. Every cause is worthwhile but some struggle for badly-needed funds.

I'd been preparing for this race since October, but had been nagged by doubts about training harder and longer. Now I was in the tent, those thoughts became a screaming in my head.

I was ready for this though; despite the noise around me, I sat in the corner, closed my eyes and concentrated on my breathing. I reminded myself of how much work I'd invested in this moment, and two minutes later I was relaxed and focused.

I knew I could finish the course at a decent speed without stopping, but how many of my four ambitions could I realistically achieve? The only one I was relatively confident of was coming in under three hours, which, although an awesome achievement, was really the only one within my own control. It was also, as far as I was concerned, the most important, so that's where my concentration was targeted.

The London course had clocks at every mile marker, so I'd carefully planned out my pace and timings. My intention was to run the first half quite hard and slow accordingly for the second. I didn't want to run an even pace in case I couldn't maintain it and slowed too much. I had confidence in my speed and endurance, and could trust the hundreds of hours I'd put in.

We were called forward and lined up at the start. I shared a few words of encouragement with a couple of first-timers, including Chris Evans. I was shivering impatiently and wanted to get going to calm the frantic butterflies in my stomach. It wasn't just the nerves that were keeping me on edge but more the weight of expectation. I knew what I'd spent months doing and what I must spend the next three hours doing but doubts come even to the most prepared. I was actually scared and kept urging the clock lower. As the moments ticked away, we all joined in with the countdown of the final ten seconds, then the klaxon blared and we were off.

The conditions were not great, as it had been raining and there's always a risk of slipping on the road. But I was experienced enough not to be worried. After all, most of my training had been done in the Welsh countryside, so it would have been more unusual for me had the weather been dry!

I kept a good pace and was happy with how the first part of the race was progressing. I passed under the halfway barrier slightly faster than I'd anticipated, but could already feel my body suffering under the extreme exertions. Just as I'd forced myself out of bed each morning with the terrifying refrain, 'Three hours, zero minutes and one second,' I motivated myself with a further phrase: 'A lifetime of joy for three hours of pain.'

Over and over I said this, to the point where I involuntarily shouted it and startled other runners around me. But they knew exactly what I meant and I'm sure it even encouraged some of their efforts too.

With eight miles to go, my feet were really hurting and I was finding it harder to lift my knees very high. My strides were shortened and my feet struck the road more often. I blocked it out and concentrated on looking ahead for the welcome arch of red and white balloons, indicating another mile completed.

I was passing Tower Bridge on the final stretch, with just under five miles to go, when I became certain I'd come in under three hours. I could reduce my pace to nearly eight minutes a mile and still make it, but I kept pushing. As a time of 2.58 sounds intentional, whereas 2.59 could just be a fluke, I owed it to my training to register at that slightly faster figure.

I passed through Parliament Square, saw the half-mile sign and turned onto The Mall. There, like a magical mirage, was the finish line. I saw the final clock had just ticked over 2.57, so I started sprinting – or at least as much as my body would allow.

Adrenalin took over and I pumped with my arms, groaning in pain. I felt the welcoming softness of the red timing mat under my feet and completed the course in 2.58.30. I've never felt so elated and exhausted at the same time.

A surprisingly heavy medal was at once hung around my neck, which almost forced me to double over as my lungs desperately sucked in as much air as possible. It had been the single most intense physical experience of my life, and I was instantly struck by a surprising wave of sadness now that it was all over.

However, I was booked in for an interview with BBC Sport, just like the previous year, and looking forward to a good plug for Shooting Star Chase. I immediately asked how the celebrity race had finished, but I'd come home third behind James Cracknell and Jenson. Still, it'd taken professional sportsmen to beat me, so I took solace in that as I stood shivering.

I waited for the interview, becoming increasingly uncomfortable as my cold, drenched kit clung to my body. After twenty minutes they told me they were just too busy and I was unceremoniously dismissed.

I was hugely disappointed and annoyed. I'd pinned a lot of hope on gaining positive publicity for the hospice charity, and wanted to say thank you to everyone who'd been involved with the marathon and supported the runners.

To be denied this when the broadcasters unceremoniously dispensed with me seemed insensitive and deflating. I thanked my Twitter followers, but that's as far as I could go. The sheer delight of running a sub-three-hour marathon (at the age of forty-five!) had been soured by a moment of indifferent officiousness.

Nevertheless, my achievement can't be taken from me, but I considered London 2015 to be the swansong of my marathon career. I didn't want to run another unless I could substantially reduce my time, and that would require many more months of intensive and dedicated training.

Inevitably though, I began to get itchy feet. After the race, Jamie and I had celebrated with several large pizzas and over the next month I gained a little weight. I didn't like this but found running without a specific aim in mind very difficult. With eleven months to go before the 2016 race, I emailed the organisers and tweeted my bold ambition. I would run again with the aim of breaking 2.50 and winning the celebrity race again. It would require that long to reach the necessary level so training has already started! As an unexpected extra, Jamie has also pledged to run the London Marathon too so no doubt we'll train and enter a few races together too.

I like having ambitious targets to work towards but also, all this running does wonders for my body and waistline. The mindset of a model is very hard to shake!

*　　*　　*

I also have the prospect of a very busy and exciting year ahead. *Eggheads* is adopting a more sedate schedule, but reports of its demise are greatly exaggerated. The programme has already notched up an incredible 1,500 episodes, which is utterly absurd but so very welcome!

The Renata Road has had some very notable attention and could garner a lot of publicity. I sincerely hope so, just to reward all the incredible blood, sweat and tears Ed Greenberg put into it. Even on a micro-budget production like this, for every person you see on screen so many more are working behind it. They gave up their time and skills free of charge in order to complete this labour of love, and that dedication deserves recognition.

I also have a few theatrical projects lined up, and am especially looking forward to performing at the Edinburgh

Festival. This is an ordeal by fire every British actor must face, but I want to keep enough space free in case that one irresistible job comes up. Yes, I'm dreaming again, but perhaps this time with an air of cautious justification.

*   *   *

I walked back to my car after signing the contract for this very book, venturing onto Oxford Street for five minutes to buy some running shorts. In that time I saw three individual young men begging, and realised nothing had changed. It was raining, they were huddled in doorways or under dripping scaffolding, and the crowds were pushing past, ignoring them.

I gave money to the first two, but my heart broke at the third who couldn't have been more than twenty. This was all in the space of a hundred metres of a single street in a very rich city. I knelt down and put my hand on his shoulder. He seemed shocked that anyone would take a real interest. I spoke to him for a minute, but then a middle-aged woman impatiently kicked at me to get by.

I totally exploded and screamed at her, in the midst of the other commuters and shoppers hurrying past. It wasn't the kick I particularly objected to, but the fact that human suffering could so easily be ignored and dismissed if it incurred a split second of minor inconvenience.

She went immediately on the defensive. She was scared and tried to make an apology, but I didn't care. I shouted at the top of my voice to make sure all and sundry heard she was an uncaring cow, who shouldn't apologise to me but to the poor soul on the street she clearly thought beneath her reckoning. She did so and gave him some money but then darted away, as my eyes seared daggers into her back.

This made me so angry. I'm bemused by how we, in such an affluent and generous country, avoid caring about those we choose not to see. Television appeals raise millions, but if we avert our eyes then it's no longer a problem.

I leant down again and asked if I could get him anything. He smilingly accepted a coffee and sandwich. I offered information about hostels, but he seemed not to want to know. I fully understood. Although I wouldn't have chosen such a terribly public place, my experience had taught me a night hostel should be avoided at all costs.

He told me his name, and I left him with my best wishes and a handshake. I so wanted to say to him, 'It gets better so please hang on,' but how could I? It was only true for me through an incredibly unlikely twist of fate, and I couldn't bring the words, which might well be lies, to my lips.

But if you're ever inclined to talk to any rough sleepers – and I beg you to do so – please ask for their names. It's a simple, humanising question that lets them know someone cares enough to see them as people, not inanimate piles of clothes or anonymous statistics.

One thing I am definitely going to do in 2015 is raise a fund to locate, house and provide for one homeless person. Yes, I'll still donate to charities and individuals, but in those cases I'll be unable to see if the help so desperately needed is really getting through.

I've been so lucky that I have a good, comfortable life now, so I owe it to my conscience to help one person and follow through to the end result. I'm in no way wealthy, but if every person who could afford it actually took this step, homelessness in this country would be eradicated overnight. We all know this and yet this tragic social problem remains, and even worsens.

* * *

I already have work booked for the summer of 2016, so hopefully my career is on an upswing. But I'll be most fascinated to see how this book is received. My publisher said, when he was first presented with the opening chapters, that he had very little interest in a book by another mediocre celebrity. We all know the type: a nonentity who foolishly thinks the public will be so fascinated by a bland life, just because he or she once had a few lines on *EastEnders*.

My own sentiments about how I'm perceived aside, I do at least hope my life has been a little more absorbing. It's not your run-of-the-mill bedtime reading, but it does have a happy and optimistic ending.

Except it's not the ending! I'm getting busier and this book marks the start of an exciting new chapter in my life. Andrew and I will get married, and I'll look at expanding my career horizons, as he's already being offered work in Hollywood.

When I think back to that cold staircase in Amsterdam central station and, more vividly, that evening in Vondelpark with the Spanish boy, I can't help feeling sad. But I marvel at how far I've come.

Yet this is no self-congratulatory pat on the back. Even though I've worked incredibly hard, I had to be given multiple chances as I childishly squandered several of them. Arthur, Rainer, Andrew and 12 Yard all gave me opportunities I could never have dreamt of, and I hope that in some small way I've repaid each of them for their kindnesses.

One of the most regular messages I get on Twitter is, 'I thought you were a smug prat on *Eggheads* but after following you on here, I've seen you're a nice, caring man.' That's lovely to read, although I'm paraphrasing with the word 'prat'.

In fact, I'm not the person on screen (do you think I'd wear those shirts in respectable society?), but merely fulfilling a role. I think it's necessary and has contributed to the success of the show. Yet I am a natural product of my life experiences, although I don't blame them for who I am. I'm a responsible adult and make my own choices now. I can only be defined by my actions today.

I hope you found my story interesting and unusual, and that it confounded your expectations. I doubt many people would guess where I came from, and indeed, I often get accused, if that's the right word, of a silver-spoon upbringing.

I didn't anticipate that writing my autobiography would be a cathartic experience, and in the main it hasn't been. I'm so far removed, both emotionally and chronologically, from most of the traumatic events I've related, and this has enabled me to look at them objectively. Of course, there's still a lot of hurt and it's certainly been difficult, but this is the first time anybody – even Andrew – will discover some of these secrets about me, so in that sense the effort was certainly worthwhile.

If I've succeeded in one thing, I hope it's in changing

preconceptions about who people really are. Every person is fighting his or her individual daily battles, and a kind word or a simple smile can make all the difference. But, whatever you are going through, please remember that it *can* get better and there's always someone who cares.

Thank you so much for the privilege of telling you my story. I can't wait to live the next chapter!